"With great joy I recommend my friend Becca Greenwood's new book, *Destined to Rule*. The first time I met Becca was at the home of her future in-laws. She and Greg were engaged to be married. Although she was an accomplished vocalist, her charismatic personality and quest for spiritual truth revealed a life calling far bigger than her singing.

"Several years after Greg and Becca were married, they moved to Houston, where Eddie and I were privileged to pastor and mentor them. Becca always wanted more of God and continually pursued purity, transparency and godliness. No matter what challenges Eddie and I presented her, she was ready and willing.

"I love this new book! Becca writes like a master strategist, explaining the original plan for humanity to rule, showing us how to overcome Satan's intimidation. She skillfully establishes God's call for us to rule as priests and kings on the earth, and she challenges us to rise up and step into our destinies.

"You may not be convinced that some authors have experienced what they have written. I assure you that Becca has. She is qualified to write *Destined to Rule*, because this is more than theory to her. I've seen her struggle, then press through and defeat darkness on many levels. My friend has moved from having a vision to lead to becoming a visionary leader! *Destined to Rule* is a unique opportunity for you to become equipped to move into your Kingdom authority. So go for it!"

—**Alice Smith**, executive director, U.S. Prayer Center

"Rebecca Greenwood is among those who keenly hear what the Spirit is saying to the churches about taking dominion. *Destined to Rule* is an outstanding, pioneering book. Not only does it clearly present the mandate for the Body of Christ to retake dominion of God's creation, but it shows practical ways that we as individuals can stand up, be counted and do our part in seeing that God's Kingdom will come."

—**C. Peter Wagner**, convening apostle, International Coalition of Apostles

"Countless Christians live in bondage to a victim mindset. They see themselves as victims of the evil schemes of Satan in this world. Rebecca Greenwood challenges this mentality with a powerful and victorious message in her book *Destined to Rule*.

"Greenwood masterfully weaves the Scriptures into real-life stories of God's intended inheritance for His children. You will be challenged to partner with God in a new way to fulfill His destiny for your life. I highly recommend *Destined to Rule* for anyone seeking to discover God's promise for a triumphant, overcoming life!"

—**Barbara Wentroble**, president and founder, International Breakthrough Ministries; author, *Prophetic Intercession; Praying with Authority; You Are Anointed;* and *Rise to Your Destiny, Woman of God*

"Not since Paul Billheimer's classic *Destined for the Throne* has a book described more clearly how believers are to pursue their destinies of authority in Christ on earth. Becca Greenwood's *Destined to Rule* is sure to become a classic in its own right."

—**Dr. Dick Eastman**, international president, Every Home for Christ

"*Destined to Rule* goes beyond mind and reason and liberates your spirit to rule with the Lord! Read this book and watch the Lord give you incredible revelation that allows you to reason, rule and reign with Him in the place where you have been called to stand."

—from the foreword by **Chuck D. Pierce**, president, Glory of Zion International Ministries, Inc.; harvest watchman, Global Harvest Ministries

"Outstanding, informative, instructive and empowering are words that captivate your mind as you read this book. Becca Greenwood has given the Body of Christ a valuable tool to enable every believer to walk in dominion and to reign in life. This is one of those must-read books for everyone's library."

—**Naomi Dowdy**, president and founder, Naomi Dowdy Ministries; resident apostle, former senior pastor, Trinity Christian Centre, Singapore

"All of us desire a sense of worth, a reason for being. If you don't know who you are, then you don't know the scope of what you can do. Rebecca Greenwood clearly establishes both, and she shows us as individuals how to fit into our own unique place in God's vast, eternal plan. *Destined to Rule* is filled with exciting and life-changing truth!"

—**Lora Allison**, founder and president, Celebration Ministries; author, *Skinned Alive: The Importance of Covering*

"Believers are called to reign in life (see Romans 5:17), but too few of us ever do. It's time we step out of passivity and make a difference in our personal worlds. *Destined to Rule* tells us how."

—**Dr. Joseph Winger**, pastor of prayer, New Life Church, Colorado Springs, Colorado

DESTINED TO
RULE

Spiritual Strategies
for Advancing
the Kingdom of God

REBECCA GREENWOOD

Chosen
Grand Rapids, Michigan

Published by Chosen Books
A division of Baker Publishing Group
P.O. Box 6287, Grand Rapids, MI 49516-6287
www.chosenbooks.com

Printed in the United States of America

Library of Congress Cataloging-in-Publication Data
Greenwood, Rebecca, 1967–
    Destined to rule : spiritual strategies for advancing the kingdom of God /
Rebecca Greenwood.
        p.   cm.
    Includes index.
    ISBN 10: 0-8007-9433-8 (pbk.)
    ISBN 978-0-8007-9433-0 (pbk.)
    1. Christian life. 2. Evangelistic work. I. Title.
    BV4501.3.G743 2007
    248.4—dc22   2007015942

To my parents, Ronnie and Mary Long, for always loving me, believing in me and teaching me to never quit. You truly instilled in me the desire, passion and commitment to be all that the Lord has created me to be. Thank you for teaching me to reach for the stars and imparting the confidence to do it.

Mom, I say thank you for the faithful, consistent and steadfast love. And for the many times throughout the years that you spoke over me that I was blessed and the Lord had a plan, I say thank you. I heard and believed.

Dad, for all the wisdom, fatherly love and gentle guidance and patience, I am forever grateful. You loved me with an earthly father's love that prepared the way for me to embrace the love of my heavenly Father.

I love you both from the bottom of my heart.

CONTENTS

1. The Original Plan for Man 19

We human beings are the special creation of God, made in His image and likeness. Adam was placed in the Garden of Eden as a spiritual son of God and the earthly representative of His Kingdom. Learn the most significant message from the Genesis 1 account of the creation of man: the divine plan for mankind, in relationship with God, to exercise dominion over creation.

2. The True King Appears 29

Adam lived in a beautiful garden, but failed. Jesus entered a dangerous wilderness and won the victory against temptation. Adam had been given the mandate of dominion over his assigned territory, but relinquished this right. Jesus came as a relational, compassionate, warring King to redeem and restore the Kingdom of God.

3. A Relationship with the King 41

Once we receive the gift of salvation through faith we have entered into the Kingdom of God and are enlisted as citizens of heaven. Discover that we are heirs of God and co-heirs with Christ in a heavenly calling. We are members of a kingly priesthood that, through the blood of Christ, now has access into the throne room and all the benefits of a kingly inheritance.

4. Creation Waits with Eager Expectation 55

When man invited evil to be at home in creation, the earth fell into the bondage of sin, corruption and decay. Creation waits eagerly for the sons of God to be revealed so that it, too, can be brought into the glorious freedom of the children of God. God desires a land of His own. It is our responsibility to redeem what Adam gave away. Creation is waiting!

FOREWORD

A timely book for this age of history has now been birthed. Rebecca Greenwood has written *Destined to Rule* for a time such as this!

One thing I have always done is read the Bible out loud to the Lord. He inspired and directed men to write the life-giving Word for us, so it is always good to read it back to Him.

Once I had planned to read Romans 6–8. I began chapter 6 and got to verse 14: "For sin shall not have dominion over you" (NKJV). I stopped abruptly and asked the Lord a question: "Lord, is this a true statement?"

I heard a voice so loud that I thought a person was standing in the room with me. The voice said, *Yes!*

I asked, "Lord, is this book completely true?"

He said, *Yes, obey My Word.*

At that moment, I knew I did not have to submit to sin as my master. I had never been taught this before in any church service I had ever attended. But at that moment a power that seemed to have had an inherited control in my family broke in my life. I knew I would never have to do what my dad had done. I did not have to fall for the same strategies Satan had used to entice my grandfather away from God's best. I knew I could walk faithfully before the Lord and be in faithful covenant with my wife and others. I came to realize that the domination of something that had been in my bloodline for generations had been detected, addressed and broken.

My life took a drastic turn from that moment on.

This is what will happen when you read this book. The concept of ruling and reigning with Christ personally and territorially is presented in such a wonderful way that you will say emphatically, "This is who I am and this is what I am to do!"

Rebecca traces God's original plan for Adam from his fall and loss to the liberation that Jesus brought mankind and all of creation. Theologically her book is wonderful yet simple! Rebecca tells us how we are positioned to rule based on the Lord's sacrifice for us.

There are times of fulfillment that God has planned in the earth realm. Heaven and earth are getting closer and closer. This creates the necessity for men and women on earth to arise to legislate God's will. We read the Bible and see men like Moses, Elijah, Daniel, Peter, Paul and John. We see women like Mary Magdalene, Deborah and Esther. Today God is raising up men and women of faith who will rule in the earth realm. He is determining new spheres of authority. These spheres are linked with assigned functions from heaven and reassigned territories on the earth.

Who will rule? "The earth is the LORD's, and the fulness thereof" (Psalm 24:1, KJV). *Fullness* means there is a place of abundance (see John 10:10). "In Him we live and move and have our being" (Acts 17:28; see Colossians 1:19, 2:9). Fullness occurs when something fills up or comes to completion (see Matthew 9:16–17; Mark 2:21–22, 6:43, 8:20). We must remember that the measure of Christ's blessing is overflowing (see Romans 15:29). Fullness is also when the salvation of the Gentiles has come into a number that satisfies God's requirement for completeness (see Romans 11:25). The Lord will complete His plan of fullness in the earth.

Who will rule the nations? "The meek . . . shall inherit the earth" (Matthew 5:5, NKJV). God will rule and we will eventually reign. Fear not! Even with the nations aligning and mounting against the God of heaven and earth, He will rule. The earth is His, and He will see to it that it is made full of His purpose and plan.

Destined to Rule helps us understand our call in the earth today. Rebecca takes us one step further in our faith. As we read, she helps us understand that we are here to do the "greater works" (John 14:12) of the Lord Jesus! Many people believe that how we use knowledge determines our power and authority in the earth. We must remember a key passage for today:

> "He shall speak pompous words against the Most High, shall persecute the saints of the Most High, and shall intend to change times and law. Then the saints shall be given into his hand for a time and times and half a time. But the court shall be seated, and they shall take away his dominion, to consume and destroy it forever. Then the kingdom and dominion, and the greatness of the kingdoms under the whole heaven, shall be given to the people, the saints of the Most High. His kingdom is an everlasting kingdom, and all dominions shall serve and obey Him."
>
> Daniel 7:25–27 (NKJV)

There will be a great struggle in the days ahead, with Satan attempting to persecute the saints by getting us out of God's timing or controlling us so we cannot enter God's timing, in part through the changing of laws around us. These laws relate primarily to how we operate in today's world and are linked with the information revolution. Many laws are being developed to stop or constrict God's children from operating in freedom. *Destined to Rule* helps the reader to return! We must return to the Lord and rule in the earth. Our society has almost removed the concept of God-consciousness from its midst through changing laws in this time. This is one of the major wars ahead for the Body of Christ. How do we rule in the midst of civil law working against us? How will we influence government without the government's removing our freedom to operate in God's Kingdom? These are key questions.

Let's return to what God said in Isaiah 1:

> Your country is desolate, your cities are burned with fire; strangers devour your land in your presence; and it is desolate, as overthrown by strangers. So the daughter of Zion is left as a booth in a vineyard, as a hut in a garden of cucumbers, as a besieged city. Unless the LORD of hosts had left to us a very small remnant, we would have become like Sodom, we would have been made like Gomorrah.... "To what purpose is the multitude of your sacrifices to Me? ... Come now, and let us reason together.... I will restore your judges as at the first, and your counselors as at the beginning."
>
> Isaiah 1:7-9, 11, 18, 26, NKJV

Destined to Rule goes beyond mind and reason and liberates your spirit to rule with the Lord! Read this book and watch the Lord give you incredible revelation that allows you to reason, rule and reign with Him in the place where you have been called to stand.

Dr. Chuck D. Pierce, president,
Glory of Zion International Ministries, Inc.
Harvest watchman, Global Harvest Ministries

ACKNOWLEDGMENTS

As I work through the final editing stages of this book, my mind begins to think of all of those who have stood with me in prayer and support of this project. I am truly grateful and blessed to have so many wonderful family members, friends and intercessors to partner with me and encourage me through the process.

First and foremost, I want to say thank you to my husband, Greg. You are my best friend and biggest support. Thank you for tirelessly researching and studying the Word of God with me through the writing of the book. Thank you for the late nights of processing and reading the freshly written pages. Thank you for being a father who willingly steps in to make sure the girls are taken care of as I work to complete the book. You are the best, and I thank God for you every day. I fully believe that the best is yet ahead for you.

To my three beautiful daughters, Kendall, Rebecca and Katie. You are my pride and joy. What exceptional young women you are! Being your mother is the most awesome assignment in my life from the Lord. I love all three of you from the bottom of my heart, and I know the Lord has a great future for each of you.

To all the intercessors who faithfully stand on the wall for me, my family and Christian Harvest International, I am forever grateful and each of you is in my prayers. Again, thank you, prayer warriors!

Sandy Christopherson, I want to especially thank you. Your heart, commitment and prayers literally undergird all the Lord has given me to do. I could not do all I do without your prayers. You are the true model of an I-1 intercessor.

To my in-laws, Jack and Pam Greenwood. Thank you for the book you placed in our hands seventeen years ago. And thank you for taking us to the conference in Dallas and inviting us to Houston for the ministry team training weekend. Our lives have never been the same. Your guidance placed Greg and me on the path the Lord has set for us. I love you both.

Ann Weinheimer, I want to express what a great joy it is to work with you. As I read the edited pages of this book, I am amazed at how smart and eloquent you make me sound. It is an honor to work with you. Thank you for doing a superb job. I look forward to our next project.

And I want to express to my Lord and heavenly Father all my heart and love. Your love is a lavish, awesome and all-consuming love. I will worship, exalt and praise You all the days of my life. To You may all glory and honor be given.

INTRODUCTION

The original, divine plan of God for mankind was dominion over creation. It was our created purpose to exert rule, authority and stewardship on the earth. Having been involved in spiritual warfare for the past sixteen years, I have watched dominion rule become a regular confession of many believers. The voice of the Church has resounded with the desire to see the manifestation and revelation of our God-given assignment of ruling and reigning.

This goal is a righteous one, but in most cases it will not be accomplished. Why not? Because it is not through confession that authority comes! Authority is inextricably tied in with responsibility. It presumes not only knowledge but rightful use of our position in Christ. It means understanding the original plan for man, walking in prayer and intimacy with the Father, walking in obedience to the Father's direction, knowing our sphere of influence and releasing dominion in our God-given assignments and territories.

Before we continue I want to point out that I am well aware of the many abuses associated with the doctrine of dominion and the negative connotations that have become coupled with it. Wrong ideology has driven a biblical mandate from God into excesses of legalism and control.

My goal is not to enter debate. It is my purpose to write a book focusing on the scriptural truths of our God-ordained assignment of dominion in order for the Church to be equipped and positioned in this strategic time in history. As believers, we may not dismiss what Scripture teaches about the original purpose of mankind simply because misconceptions exist. We cannot allow the enemy to continue to steal the purpose of our existence. Let's not throw out the baby with the bathwater!

The original mandate that we are to rule, have dominion and steward the land is stated in Genesis 1:28: "God blessed them and said to them, 'Be fruitful and increase in number; fill the earth and subdue it. Rule over the fish of the sea and the birds of the air and over every living creature that moves on the ground.'" For centuries the enemy has established strongholds in every area of life to thwart this mandate. Many of us in the Body of Christ have come to realize that we are called to war against this demonic scheme. We are not supposed to live as victims cowering before a cloud of darkness, but as victors partnering with the Lord in our created purpose and destiny.

I have warred and will continue to war against the defilement and bondage established by the enemy; it is the Church's responsibility to do so. But I perceive that the Lord is changing our stance in this war. He is challenging us to discover our legal place of ruling and reigning as Kingdom ambassadors. By walking in our authority, we spread the message of the Kingdom of God, draw the lost world to the

God we serve, establish righteousness in the land and usher forth spiritual and social transformation.

Within each of us is a longing to be part of something great. We all experience thoughts or even buried passions of wanting to be involved in a bigger plan—a plan in which the rule of darkness is shattered by goodness and truth. God placed that desire within us. We no longer have to feel as if our lives have little meaning. We, you and I, have been chosen and positioned for the purpose of setting forth the righteous standard—one that will cause the world to take notice.

Friend, it is not a mistake that you are alive during this time in history. God ordained you and me to partner with Him at this particular time to see His Kingdom restored in the earth. It is my prayer that as we explore the Word of God together in the pages of *Destined to Rule*, you and I—heirs to His Kingdom—will discern the Lord's intent for His creation.

1

THE ORIGINAL PLAN FOR MAN

Have you sensed how the search for meaning in life is expanding in today's world? The desire for purpose and destiny is probably unparalleled. For Christians this means that the opportunities to reach out with the supernatural power of God and influence our culture are laden with fruit. Researchers tell us, in fact, that more souls have come into the Kingdom of God in the last two decades than in all the centuries combined since Christ's ministry on earth. These souls have found the Savior—and the answers they were seeking.

But this does not mean that the battle against darkness is easing. Statistics also point to the probability that only *4 percent* of today's youth will embrace evangelical Christianity.

This raises a troubling question: If we have the answers to life's questions, why are we still so ineffective in reaching vast numbers of people—including the next generation?

We are entering what the Bible calls the fullness of time, and much is at stake. God is positioning us to understand how we can advance His Kingdom into every realm. held captive by darkness. In order for us to understand where we are going, however, we have to understand where we came from. Let's take a few moments to review our reason for being here on earth—the true meaning of life.

Made in God's Image

God had a specific plan in mind when He created man:

God said, Let Us [Father, Son, and Holy Spirit] make mankind in Our image, after Our likeness, and let them have complete authority over the fish of the sea, the birds of the air, the [tame] beasts, and over all of the earth, and over everything that creeps upon the earth. So God created man in His own image, in the image and likeness of God He created him; male and female He created them. And God blessed them and said to them, Be fruitful, multiply, and fill the earth, and subdue it [using all its vast resources in the service of God and man]; and have dominion over the fish of the sea, the birds of the air, and over every living creature that moves upon the earth.

Genesis 1:26–28, AMP

We human beings, both men and women, are the special creation of God, made in His image and likeness. No other part of creation can make that claim. The Hebrew word for *image* is *selem*, which refers to a representation of the Deity, meaning we are the pattern, model and example of the image of God in the earth. The Hebrew word for *likeness* is *demut*, which means "something that looks like or resembles something else." This is the only passage in Scripture in which both words are coupled together. The Lord was communicating an important message in this word structure. He was saying that we are the *likeness-image* of God. Not only are we *representative*, but we are *representational*. Man is the spokesperson, diplomat, agent, courier, commissioner and ambassador of the Kingdom of God. Man was created as the adequate, faithful, visible, tangible, physical representative of God in the earth.

God is revealed in Scripture as a personal heavenly Father, one who created Adam and Eve in order to be in relationship with them. In Genesis 1, the general name of God, Elohim, is used, which emphasizes His greatness and power. In Genesis 2:4, another name for God is introduced: Yahweh, or Lord. This is the personal and covenant name through which God reveals Himself to His people. Central in the revelation of God's covenant name of Yahweh is His loving kindness, His redemptive concern for mankind and His faithful presence alongside His people. This personal mention of God is used when He is in direct relationship with His people and creation. When the two names are linked together, Yahweh Elohim, or Lord God, they signify that our God is an all-powerful Creator who has entered into a caring, loving relationship with mankind.

Let's look briefly at the origins of this relationship and the reason the devil went to such lengths to destroy it.

God Builds a Relationship

God formed Adam "from the dust of the ground and breathed into his nostrils the breath of life, and the man became a living being" (Genesis 2:7). This expression of the Father was unique in all of His creation. By lovingly imparting His very breath to give man life, God confirmed that humankind holds a higher position than the rest of creation.

The triune God—Father, Son and Holy Spirit—imparted to man a triune nature: body, soul and spirit. The human body, by virtue of being shaped and formed from the dust of the earth, has a special relation to it; we might say that it is our world consciousness. Through the body's five senses—sight, sound, touch, smell and taste—we live in and interact with all that exists around us.

The body houses the spirit and soul. When God took the dust of the earth and "breathed into his nostrils the breath of life," Adam was no longer an empty shell but a man brought to life by the Spirit of God. The Hebrew word for *life* is *chaim*, which is plural in form and is interpreted as "lives." Derek Prince explains this in *War in Heaven* (Chosen Books, 2003):

> God breathed into Adam the breath of "lives." We find, as we go on throughout Scripture, that there are various forms of life: spiritual life and physical life, mortal life and immortal life. All these concepts are contained in seed form in this chapter of Genesis and developed in the subsequent unfolding of Scripture.

A similar process occurs when we receive the gift of salvation. When we are "born again," God breathes His life and Spirit into us. Our "spirit-man" is now alive and gives us God-consciousness. It is through the spirit that God speaks to us. As we worship, pray and spend time in the Word of God, our spirits are cultivated and grow. It is God's design that the body and soul walk in submission to the spirit.

The creation of Adam's body and the spirit that God breathed into him brought about this result: "And the man became a living being." The soul is composed of the mind, will and emotions; it allows self-consciousness. The soul was designed to walk in submission to the spirit so that we might follow God's will in all areas of our lives.

Adam was now fully formed to live in the wonderful creation around him. But God pointed out to this new being that he was not yet complete: The man had no suitable helper. We know the wonderful story of how God caused Adam to fall asleep, removed one of his ribs and closed up the place with flesh. Then from that rib the Lord fashioned a woman (translated "of man") and introduced her to Adam. (See Genesis 2:20–22.)

The Lord formed woman from Adam's own body to illustrate that she was not inferior to man but was his bone and flesh. They were partners who were called to rule together.

There is a special relationship between divine life and human life. God gave Adam and Eve—and us, their descendants—the power of choice regarding fellowship with Him. The man and woman enjoyed their closeness with the Lord and reflected His love, glory and holiness. Morally, man was sinless. He was also wise and eager to walk in obedience to the Lord.

Adam Discovers His Calling

The divine plan for mankind was this:

God blessed them and said to them, Be fruitful, multiply, and fill the earth, and subdue it [using all its vast resources in the service of God and man]; and have dominion over

23

the fish of the sea, the birds of the air, and over every living creature that moves upon the earth.

Genesis 1:28, AMP

By virtue of having made man in His image, God had endowed the earth's new caretaker with intellect, creative abilities and an inherent gift of leadership to rule and reign. Our Father is always about the business of His Kingdom and created man with the same calling and design. It was a natural consequence, therefore, that man be given the responsibility to steward, or manage, creation. This included the earth and all living creatures upon it.

In order to understand this mandate, we have to understand the commands *subdue* and *have dominion*. The Hebrew word for *subdue* is *kabas*, meaning "to bring into subjection, to dominate." It suggests that the party being subdued is hostile to the subduer, requiring some sort of force if the subduing is to occur successfully. Genesis 1:28 implies, therefore, that creation was not willing to do man's bidding, but man would have to bring creation into order by using his strength. Creation is not to rule man.

The Hebrew word for *dominion* is *radah*, which refers not to God's rule and responsibility but to man's. It means "to manage or reign from a position of sovereignty." This exalted position of man is outlined in Psalm 8:4–8:

What is man that you are mindful of him, the son of man that you care for him? You made him a little lower than the heavenly beings and crowned him with glory and honor. You made him ruler over the works of your hands; you put everything under his feet: all flocks and herds, and the beasts of the field, the birds of the air, and the fish of the sea, all that swim the paths of the seas.

We humans were made for a glorious purpose: God fashioned us to share His own authority over part of His creation. World dominion was to be the role of man, along with its incredible privileges and weighty responsibilities. Adam was directed to live and move in a kingly manner over the earth. Dominion was his birthright and his pleasure.

A Snake in the Grass

Into this perfect world came one who craved that dominion for himself. Having already lost his battle to overthrow God, Satan set into motion his evil scheme to destroy that which our Lord held most precious—His creation and humanity. If Satan could not capture the high place of God in the universe, he would try to gain at least earthly authority.

The devil schemed, therefore, to deceive and tempt man to rebel against God and, thus, by man's forfeiture, gain control in the earth. And as we know all too well, he succeeded. Fewer words in Scripture are sadder than the opening verses of Genesis 3, which tell the story of the serpent's beguiling Eve to look at the fruit tree in the middle of the Garden with new eyes:

> When the woman saw that the tree was good (suitable, pleasant) for food and that it was delightful to look at, and a tree to be desired in order to make one wise, she took of its fruit and ate; and she gave some also to her husband, and he ate. Then the eyes of them both were opened.
>
> Genesis 3:6–7, AMP

The effects of their rebellion against God—their willful disobedience of His commands for governing the earth— manifested immediately. Physical, spiritual and moral death

25

gripped their lives. Even though they would live for many years, they would experience physical death through which their bodies would return to the dust of the ground out of which they were formed. Morally, their intimate trust with God was destroyed as their nature became sinful. Before sinning, their nakedness caused no shame. But after eating fruit from the Tree of Knowledge of Good and Evil, their nakedness became a sign of disgrace. Spiritually, they experienced a separation in their relationship with God. Instead of being drawn to commune with their Creator, Adam and Eve were now uncomfortable in His presence as they could feel His displeasure. They hid from Him. Sin separated them from the intimate communion they had so freely and gloriously experienced before their act of rebellion.

From this time, Satan has waged a relentless battle of deception against mankind, tempting us to believe we can be like God and, therefore, determine for ourselves what is good and evil. This has fostered an independent spirit in humanity by which God's Word is rejected as the infallible verdict by which we are to live. Mankind has become his own false god. It is due to this satanic deception that many people believe they can live immoral lives and still experience eternal salvation. And deception will be the primary weapon against humanity to open the way for embracing the Antichrist.

God Deals with Sin

God told Adam and Eve the results of their sin. For Eve, the consequences involved her immediate family: pain in childbirth and a new kind of submission to her husband, who would now "rule over you" (Genesis 3:16). To Adam, provision from the earth would now come by the sweat of his brow until death claimed his body. The land that was created for prosperity would now struggle to produce.

> "Cursed is the ground because of you; through painful toil you will eat of it all the days of your life. It will produce thorns and thistles for you, and you will eat the plants of the field. By the sweat of your brow you will eat your food until you return to the ground, since from it you were taken; for dust you are and to dust you will return."
>
> Genesis 3:17–19

The punishments placed on man and woman, along with the effect on nature, were meant to be a reminder of the consequences of sin. Banished from their beautiful Garden, Adam and Eve learned to depend on God in the midst of trials and hardship.

The Lord also dealt with the serpent, Satan, because of his deceiving scheme. But in the midst of the curse, God released His plan of redemption, the new covenant to be established through Jesus:

> So the LORD God said to the serpent, "Because you have done this, cursed are you above all the livestock and all the wild animals! You will crawl on your belly and you will eat dust all the days of your life. And I will put enmity between you and the woman, and between your offspring and hers; he will crush your head, and you will strike his heel."
>
> Genesis 3:14–15

Our God is a loving Father. In the midst of Satan's supposed victory of deception, God prophesied His plan of redemption for lost humanity: While Satan would strike at the heel of Jesus, the offspring of woman, Jesus would batter and crush Satan's head. Satan's defeat and destruction were pronounced and the plan of redemption was decreed during the breaking and destruction of the original covenant.

The Effect of Sin on Humanity

The disobedience of the man and woman resulted in the introduction of the law of sin and death to the entire human race. Scripture does not tell us that all sinned when Adam sinned or that his guilt was attributed to all of humanity. His rebellion did, however, open the door for all of us to be born with a sinful human nature, with the inbred desire to go our own way without consideration of God and His leading in our lives. The good news is, our Father will not allow Satan the ultimate victory through his deception in the Garden of Eden. He sent the true King to break the curse of the Fall and to redeem mankind.

It might appear that man's original mandate was lost or at least skewed in this interchange in the Garden. We know that the call for men and women to reign will not find its ultimate expression until the Lord returns and establishes His Kingdom. But what about the meantime? We find the answer in the reason Jesus came to earth as a human being, the subject of the next chapter.

2

❀❀❀❀❀❀❀❀❀❀❀❀❀❀❀❀❀❀❀❀❀❀❀❀❀

THE TRUE KING APPEARS

God did not forget His covenant plan for mankind. Adam was created to have dominion over the earth, to serve as a kingly representative of God over this part of creation. When he failed, God sent His Son, Jesus, to save humanity from its lost state. Jesus laid down His heavenly robes to walk the earth and restore that which was forfeited by Adam and Eve. He came as servant, priest, deliverer, savior and redeemer to defeat and strip Satan of his dominion over our lives and to position us to partner with God once again in releasing the Kingdom of God on the earth.

In order to understand how Jesus destroyed the power of death and the impact this has on our regaining dominion over the earth, let's take a few moments to study His life.

Jesus Is Tempted

We read in Matthew 3 that Jesus came from Galilee to the Jordan for the purpose of being baptized by John the Baptist. This was the start of Jesus' public ministry, and the Father blessed Him with visible and audible signs: As soon as Jesus came up from the water, the heavens opened, the Holy Spirit descended on Him in the form of a dove and God's voice announced, "This is my Son, whom I love; with him I am well pleased" (verse 17).

Before being fully released into His earthly ministry, however, Jesus had to face the enemy's fiercest temptations. He had to succeed where Adam and Eve failed. Thus "Jesus was led by the Spirit into the desert to be tempted by the devil" (Matthew 4:1). It is sensible to imagine that Jesus spent these days in prayer and meditation on God's Word for the work His Father had sent Him to accomplish. And day after day He fasted. Just like Moses and Elijah before Him (see Exodus 34:28; 1 Kings 19:8), Jesus fasted for forty days and forty nights. Moses, the lawgiver, received the two tablets of the Testimony after his fasting; Elijah, a great and dramatic prophet, learned to hear the still, small voice of God after his fasting. Jesus' fast marked the culmination of the Law and the prophets, and the beginning of a new covenant.

The First Temptation

At the end of the fasting period, Satan wasted no time in trying to lure Jesus into sin. Scripture records three temptations, each with an underlying threat to Jesus' identity. The first temptation, to procure food by turning stones into bread, took advantage of Jesus' hunger.

Notice Satan's wording at the outset of this temptation: "If you are the Son of God . . ." (Matthew 4:3). This recalled the words spoken from heaven at Jesus' baptism. By using the word *if*, Satan was not questioning that Jesus was the Son of God. Instead he was saying, "*Since* you are the Son of God, take this opportunity to show it by commanding that stones be turned into bread." Satan was attempting to seduce Jesus into negating His identification as the Son of Man by meeting His personal needs in a way that man cannot. Jesus refused to use His power in His own interests. He responded by proclaiming words from Scripture: Man is not dependent upon bread alone for life; rather, God is the source of life.

The Second Temptation

After hearing Jesus quote the Word of God in order to repel him, Satan himself turned to Scripture—Psalm 91—in his second temptation. As we will see below, Satan is fully able to quote Scripture. Being the father of lies, however, he will misuse the intent of the verses in order to deceive, control and confuse.

Satan led Jesus to the highest point of the Temple in Jerusalem. Notice how this temptation followed the same pattern as that experienced by Adam and Eve. Satan can usually achieve victory if he can trick a person into drawing false conclusions. Recall his words to Eve: "Did God really say . . . ?" Likewise the enemy tried to tempt Jesus into testing the truth of God's Word by convincing Him to jump from the heights of the Temple. "If You are really the Son of God," said the taunting voice, "then would You not be rescued by angels?" It is believed that the location of this temptation took place at the southeastern corner of the wall overlooking the Kidron Valley. Satan may also have been tempting Jesus with the fact that the people below, seeing His miraculous protection from this high jump, would accept Him immediately.

31

Jesus did not deny the truth of the words from Psalm 91: He began His response by saying, "It is *also* written" (Matthew 4:7, emphasis added). But He aligned those words with the further truth that one must not put the Lord God to a test. The Greek word for *tempt* or *test* in this usage is *ekpeiraseis*, and it means "to test in order to see how far one can go or how much one can get away with." Satan was attempting to interfere with Jesus' relationship with His Father. A demand for proof from God would be an expression of a lack of faith and trust. Jesus did not succumb.

The Third Temptation

In his third challenge, Satan took Jesus to a high mountain and "showed him all the kingdoms of the world and their splendor. 'All this I will give you,' he said, 'if you will bow down and worship me'" (verses 8–9).

This was obviously a supernatural experience. Luke 4:5 states: "The devil led him up to a high place and showed him in an *instant* all the kingdoms of the world" (emphasis added). The Greek word used for *instant* is *stigme*. This is the only time this word is used in the New Testament. It is akin to one second of time or tick of the clock. This shows us that Jesus and Satan were dealing not only with the physical realm of the earth but also the spiritual. And, of course, the conflict continues in both realms today.

But we also know that Jesus is sovereign ruler over all creation as stated in Daniel 7:14:

He was given authority, glory and sovereign power; all peoples, nations and men of every language worshiped him. His dominion is an everlasting dominion that will not pass away, and his kingdom is one that will never be destroyed.

Even so, in this third attempt Satan tried to establish his own dominion in the earth by challenging Jesus to worship him. Jesus recognized that as far as the earth is concerned, Satan had become the "prince of this world" (John 12:31), due to Adam's forfeiting of dominion. As a result Satan was authorized to exert rule that rightfully belonged to mankind and the Creator.

Bowing to Satan would have been an admission that Jesus was aligning Himself with fallen mankind. It would have been an act of disobedience and rebellion to His Father's plan of restoration. Jesus would have fallen as Adam and Eve had fallen. He refused the offer, by stating that God is the only one to be worshiped and served.

Satan tempted Jesus in all three areas He was sent to earth to restore. Satan first tempted Jesus in His humanity by addressing the physical area of hunger. Jesus came to restore the fallen nature of mankind by offering salvation to those who would believe. Satan then confronted Jesus at a place of worship. Jesus came to restore mankind's broken relationship with the Father. Lastly, Satan proceeded to convince Jesus to follow him by promising to give Him the kingdoms of the world—an action that, conversely, would have elevated Satan to greater supremacy. Jesus' purpose in coming to earth was to defeat the enemy and restore man's lost rule and dominion, establishing the Kingdom of heaven in the earth. Unlike Adam, who lived in a beautiful garden and failed, Jesus entered a dangerous wilderness and won the victory against temptation.

The Kingdom of Heaven Is Near

After Jesus emerged from the wilderness, He embarked on His earthly ministry. The Kingdom of God was His focus, as shown in His early teaching: "Repent, for the kingdom of heaven is near" (Matthew 4:17). Many of us interpret this as coming in the near future, but that is not the correct meaning. The Greek word for *near* is *engliken*, indicating that the Kingdom has drawn near or, in other words, is present.

This affects the life of the Church, certainly, and her calling to reach into the darkness to save lost souls. But it also means that the cause of creation is championed. God, through His Kingdom rule on earth, is revealing Himself powerfully in all His works. As Kingdom authority is exerted, Satan and his followers are filled with terror. There is a great clash of wills over the question of submitting to God's rule.

We saw in chapter 1 that Adam was created to rule and have dominion on the earth—a kingly position by virtue of representing the Kingdom of God. And not only was he representative, but he was also representational—meaning that everything he accomplished until the Fall was a manifestation of the Kingdom of God.

The same was true of Jesus: He represented the Kingdom of God, also called the Kingdom of heaven. His purpose was to come as King to establish His rule and government. His teachings and parables explained truths of this Kingdom and how to obtain an inheritance in it. Jesus was also representational. Fully God and fully man, He moved in Kingdom authority.

Jesus did not come to form a religion but to establish relationship. Throughout His ministry on earth, Jesus was confronted by the religious leaders of the time, the Sadducees and Pharisees, who were so bound by Jewish tradition and the Law they could not see its fulfillment.

So Jesus proved time and time again that He was a compassionate and mighty Savior, one who was compelled to meet the needs of His children and make a way for a new and better covenant. Healing the man with the withered hand, redirecting the hard hearts of those who brought a woman to Him who had been caught in the act of adultery, raising the dead, feeding thousands who were hungry for more than just food, Jesus showed with every encounter that the Kingdom extends compassion, kindness and patience in order to bring about repentance. Those He touched found forgiveness and salvation; His accusers were left speechless by His authority and assertion of power. His word released the Kingdom of heaven into every situation, and in every instance the result was dominion over sin and death.

> And you who were dead in trespasses and in the uncircumcision of your flesh (your sensuality, your sinful carnal nature), [God] brought to life together with [Christ], having [freely] forgiven us all our transgressions, having cancelled and blotted out and wiped away the handwriting of the note (bond) with its legal decrees and demands which was in force and stood against us (hostile to us). This [note with its regulations, decrees, and demands] He set aside and cleared completely out of our way by nailing it to [His] cross.
>
> Colossians 2:13–14, AMP

The Law did not give life or the power to obey God; Jesus came to set us free from the slavery of sin, restoring our rightful position before God. Once Jesus is alive in our hearts, His laws are put into our minds and written on our hearts, giving us the desire, strength and authority to move as kingly representatives on the earth.

The King as Priest

When Adam sinned, mankind was separated from God. It was not until Jesus' atoning death that we were restored. In the centuries before Jesus' appearing, however, God made a way for sin to be dealt with. He established the role of the priest, whose office in the old covenant involved a system of sacrificial offerings as propitiation for sin—and foreshadowed the perfect sacrifice Jesus would make on the cross. The word *priest* in Latin means "bridge builder."

John tells us that the "Word became flesh and made his dwelling among us. We have seen his glory, the glory of the One and Only, who came from the Father, full of grace and truth" (John 1:14). The Greek word for *dwelt* is *skenoo,* which means "to tent or encamp." Some translations say that the Word became flesh and tabernacled with us. Jesus was God's representative here on earth; He was also the meeting place for God and man. In other words, not only was Jesus the tabernacle and the priest of the tabernacle, He was also the sacrificing High Priest and the sacrifice. He became our substitute.

After Jesus took upon Himself the punishment for sin, He entered heaven, where He serves as High Priest on behalf of mankind.

> The point of what we are saying is this: We do have such a high priest, who sat down at the right hand of the throne of the Majesty in heaven, and who serves in the sanctuary, the true tabernacle set up by the Lord, not by man.
>
> Hebrews 8:1–2

This was Jesus' redemptive purpose in functioning as our High Priest.

> But as it now is, He [Christ] has acquired a [priestly] ministry which is as much superior and more excellent [than the old] as the covenant (the agreement) of which He is the Mediator (the Arbiter, Agent) is superior and more excellent, [because] it is enacted and rests upon more important (sublimer, higher, and nobler) promises.
>
> verse 6, AMP

Jesus was the mediator of a better covenant because it was built on higher promises. A superior messenger and a superior priesthood mean a superior covenant.

The Priest as King

The Jews expected their Messiah to come as a warrior. They longed for a savior who would initiate a political revolution against the stranglehold of the Roman Empire. They envisioned a warrior-king who would conquer their enemies just as King David had.

Jesus came as King, as we have established, but He did not come to lead a political revolution or to war against the physical kingdoms of the earth. He came to establish the government of God by warring against and defeating Satan, who held a stranglehold of sin and death. By His sinless life and sacrificial death, He took back the dominion given to Satan. "Jesus approached [His disciples] and, breaking the silence, said to them, All authority (all power of rule) in heaven and on earth has been given to Me" (Matthew 28:18, AMP).

Jesus restored all that had been stolen and reclaimed His territory. The Greek word for *authority* is *exousia*. It means "rightful, actual and unimpeded power to act, possess, control or dispose of someone or something." The enemy and all of his demonic forces and satanic powers of the world are now disarmed, and the curse of the Fall is reversed: "And having disarmed the powers and authorities, he made a public spectacle of them, triumphing over them by the cross" (Colossians 2:15).

The word *disarmed* is also translated *stripped*. Jesus stripped the power of Satan to hold mankind bound to the dominion of sin. Christ triumphed, and the entire rule and power and authority over all of Satan's plans, authorities, dominions and powers were given to Him.

By having the eyes of your heart flooded with light, so that you can know and understand the hope to which He has called you, and how rich is His glorious inheritance in the saints (His set-apart ones), and [so that you can know and understand] what is the immeasurable and unlimited and surpassing greatness of His power in and for us who believe, as demonstrated in the working of His mighty strength, which He exerted in Christ when He raised Him from the dead and seated Him at His [own] right hand in the heavenly [places], far above all rule and authority and power and dominion and every name that is named [above every title that can be conferred], not only in this age and in this world, but also in the age and the world which are to come. And He has put all things under His feet and has appointed Him the universal and supreme Head of the church [a headship exercised throughout the church], which is His body, the fullness of Him Who fills all in all [for in that body lives the full measure of Him Who makes everything complete, and Who fills everything everywhere with Himself].

Ephesians 1:18–23, AMP

Jesus took back the authority that Adam and Eve relinquished and established the government of God in the earth and spiritual realm. He was, in fact, the first man since Adam who walked the earth as a true carrier of dominion—authoritative, supernatural power in the earth. He models for us what dominion over creation looks like. He calmed the storm and walked on water. He multiplied food. He told the disciples where to cast their nets in order to receive a great catch. He rebuked a fig tree when it did not produce food for Him. Even in His death, the curtain of the Temple was torn from top to bottom, the earth shook, rocks split, tombs broke open and the bodies of many holy people who had previously died were raised to life. All of earth was subject to Jesus, the Son of Man. As we will discuss in depth later, those who receive Him as Lord and Savior are rightly positioned to stand on the earth as ambassadors, ruling and reigning in their assigned territories, and extending and establishing the Kingdom of heaven in the earth.

When Will the Kingdom Be Established?

Scripture says that Jesus will return to build a new earth and heaven.

While He was seated on the Mount of Olives, the disciples came to Him privately and said, Tell us, when will this take place, and what will be the sign of Your coming and of the end (the completion, the consummation) of the age? Jesus answered them, Be careful that no one misleads you [deceiving you and leading you into error]. For many will come in (on the strength of) My name [appropriating the name which belongs to Me], saying, I am the Christ (the Messiah), and they will lead many astray. And you will hear of wars and rumors of wars; see that you are not frightened or troubled, for this must take place, but the end is not yet. For nation will rise against nation, and kingdom against kingdom, and there will be famines and earthquakes in place after place; all this is but the beginning [the early pains] of the birth pangs [of the intolerable anguish]. Then they will hand you over to suffer affliction and tribulation and put you to death, and you will be hated by all nations for My name's sake. And then many will be offended and repelled and will begin to distrust and desert [Him Whom they ought to trust and obey] and will stumble and fall away and betray one another and pursue one another with hatred. And many false prophets will rise up and deceive and lead many into error. And the love of the great body of people will grow cold because of the multiplied lawlessness and iniquity, but he who endures to the end will be saved. And this good news of the kingdom (the Gospel) will be preached throughout the whole world as a testimony to all the nations, and then will come the end.

Matthew 24:3–14, AMP

In the above verses the Lord spoke of wars, rumors of war, famine, earthquakes, nation against nation, kingdom against kingdom. As Jesus referred to these events, He stated that these signs are the beginning of the birth pangs of His return. I believe this is the time in which we are living; however, we have to be cautious about stating that the end is upon us as we witness these events unfolding on the earth. Yes, they serve as signs, but Jesus explained that the end will come when the Good News of the Kingdom has been preached throughout the whole world to all nations. This directive to go disciple the nations includes not just the people of those nations, but the land, government, leaders, rulers, businesses, families, schools and so on.

This is vital for us to comprehend, because it affects the timing of the return of Jesus. Not the hour, but the timing. As Jesus explained in Matthew 24:36, only the Father knows the exact day and hour: "But of that [exact] day and hour no one knows, not even the angels of heaven, nor the Son, but only the Father" (AMP).

We have, nonetheless, a role in the fulfillment of the Lord's return. This is where we, as believers and followers of Christ, come into the big picture. By fulfilling our directive to reach all nations of the world with the Good News, we have a part in determining when the stage is set for the return of the Lord. This is the very essence of our dominion mandate, the purpose for establishing and extending the Kingdom of God.

Let's move ahead now and explore our relationship with our King and learn more about the exciting purpose for which each of us has been created.

3

A Relationship with the King

It was 1990. I was in my early twenties and a new mother. My husband, Greg, and I were the youth pastors of a church in Denton, Texas. We were happily serving the Lord as He was touching the lives of the young people He had assigned to us for that season. Even so, we were experiencing an increasing desire to know Him more.

My husband's parents had been pastors for many years, and we noticed that God was doing a new and deeper work in their lives. We saw newfound joy and passion in their walks with the Lord. It made us curious. So when they invited us to an upcoming conference about drawing close to God and hearing His voice, we accepted. We were curious, but also a little cautious and skeptical. After all, we had never been to a Christian event where hearing the voice of the Lord was discussed.

The conference was intimidating and captivating at the same time. I had always felt the Lord leading me in my life and had an "inner knowing" that He had created me for a purpose, but I did not know what it was. Now, for the first time, I was hearing explanations of what I had experienced even as a young child. I had been hearing the voice of God and His direction in my life, but my experience was limited.

As the event came to an end, the conference leaders offered to pray for those in attendance who desired a deeper relationship with the Lord and felt His leading concerning a call and purpose. Greg and I instantly and simultaneously rose to our feet. The leaders then prayed for those standing, asking God to touch us in a new way. They prayed that we would have ears to hear His voice and respond to His purpose and calling. During the ministry time, I felt the presence of the Lord tangibly. It was a presence full of peace, grace, comfort and love. It was wonderful and left me hungering for more.

As we left the building, a friend of my in-laws whom I had never met approached us. She asked if I was Rebecca. I said yes. She introduced herself to me and said that earlier that afternoon the Lord had given her my name and a prophetic word. She had to explain to me what a prophetic word was as I had never heard of such a thing. I thought to myself, *Lord, this is a fast answer to the prayer that was just prayed over me at the conference. Actually, You answered the prayer before I even prayed it!* I was overcome with gratitude that He had heard my heart's cry.

In the prophetic message the Lord called me by name. As the woman spoke the words He had given her to share with me, I felt as well as heard that He was calling me closer to Himself and into a season of understanding His love and purpose for my life. It was both tender and powerful, and it sparked an intense desire and hunger to draw close to the Lord. That night was the beginning of my desire to walk with Him in a new measure of understanding and authority.

My father-in-law, Jack Greenwood, observing the increased hunger for the Lord that Greg and I were experiencing, gave us a book that explained the importance of a relationship with the Holy Spirit. This was a life-changing event for both of us. As I read the pages, I felt the Lord's presence resting on me. I could not wait to arrive home in the evening to read. What else was I about to learn and encounter?

As I finished the book, I knelt down and prayed the prayer printed at the end, inviting the Holy Spirit to fill me. Instantly I felt a powerful and all-consuming presence flood over me from the top of my head to the soles of my feet. I was embraced in the presence of the Spirit and felt Him filling my spirit to overflowing. I was overcome; I had never felt anything so wonderful. I prayed, "Lord, please don't let this presence ever leave me."

After several minutes, the Lord showed me a vision. Amazed to be receiving such clear revelation from the Lord, I sat quiet and still. He was speaking to me, and I knew His voice. My heart raced, and tears streamed down my face.

In the vision I was standing on a platform surrounded by thousands and thousands of people. They were extending their hands to touch mine, and I was reaching out to touch each of them. I was reaching for as many hands as I could.

I did not understand what this meant. I asked, "What is this You are showing me?"

He answered with a question: *Becca, will you be accountable for the souls I have assigned to you? Will you reach them for Me?* I did not understand the fullness of what He was asking me. I did know at that moment, however, that the Lord had put His hand on Greg and me and that our lives were going to change quickly. He had a purpose for us, and we needed training. I responded the only way I knew: "Yes, Lord, show me how."

That experience has been a driving inspiration in my life of serving the Lord. And as I grow in Him, more revelation comes about how each one of us is called to fulfill our responsibilities here as Kingdom representatives.

Holy Spirit–Led

You see, if you are a son or daughter of the King, your life is ministry. Everything about you is ministry. Everywhere you go—at home, the workplace, school, church, your neighborhood, the grocery store—you are a minister of the Kingdom of heaven. You are never on vacation from this assignment. It is a constant state of being.

The gospel of Luke tells us that "Jesus returned to Galilee in the *power of the Spirit*, and news about him spread through the whole countryside" (4:14, emphasis added). In Matthew Jesus is quoted as saying that He drove out demons "by the Spirit of God" (12:28). Jesus is our perfect example in living out this Kingdom walk, and we can be encouraged that the Holy Spirit, who empowered and worked through Him, guides us as well.

Jesus has promised the gift of the Holy Spirit to all who ask: "You will receive power when the Holy Spirit comes on you; and you will be my witnesses in Jerusalem, and in all Judea and Samaria, and to the ends of the earth" (Acts 1:8). The anointing of the Holy Spirit gives us the boldness and power we need in order to accomplish mighty works in Christ's name and to make our witness and proclamation an effective one.

This is because, as amazing as it sounds, as sons of God we are also partakers of His divine nature:

> His divine power has given us everything we need for life and godliness through our knowledge of him who called us by his own glory and goodness. Through these he has given us his very great and precious promises, so that through them you may participate in the divine nature and escape the corruption in the world caused by evil desires.
>
> 2 Peter 1:3–4

When we trust Jesus as our Savior, the Holy Spirit comes to live within us, positioning us as participants in the nature of God. A slave to the law does not have the divine nature of the Father, but only the realization of a desperate need for God. But as sons, through the infilling of the Holy Spirit, we can cry out, "Abba, Father!"

It is through relationship with our Savior and the seal of the Holy Spirit that we grow and mature in our spiritual walks. But we also have position: Once we receive the gift of salvation through faith in Jesus Christ, we are enlisted as citizens of heaven and sons and daughters of God. And as sons and daughters, we are also heirs. Let's explore further the authority and benefits of these positions.

Living as "Sons of God"

As we have noted, the only way to come into the family of God is through regeneration, or salvation, in Jesus Christ. As this occurs, one of the blessings bestowed on us is adoption into the family of God: We are given the unfathomable privilege of becoming His sons and daughters. Paul refers to this in two of his letters: "He predestined us to be adopted as his sons through Jesus Christ, in accordance with his pleasure and will" (Ephesians 1:5); "To purchase the freedom of (to ransom, to redeem, to atone for) those who were subject to the Law, that we might be adopted and have sonship conferred upon us [and be recognized as God's sons]" (Galatians 4:5, AMP).

Adopted with Adult Status

The New Testament word for *adoption* is *huiothesian*, which means "to position as an adult son." Not only are we adopted into God's family, we enjoy all the privileges and responsibilities of adult sonship. In the following excerpt from *The Bible Exposition Commentary* (Victor Books, 1996), Warren W. Wiersbe explains this concept:

> We are the children of God by faith in Christ, born into God's family. But every child of God is automatically placed into the family as a son, and as a son he has all the legal rights and privileges of a son. When a sinner trusts Christ and is saved, as far as his condition is concerned, he is a "spiritual babe" who needs to grow (1 Peter 2:2–3); but as far as his position is concerned, he is an adult son who can draw on the Father's wealth and who can exercise all the wonderful privileges of sonship.

This is a powerful statement of our position as sons and daughters of God. We do not have to wait to enjoy the spiritual riches we have in Christ. Paul teaches:

> Now what I mean is that as long as the inheritor (heir) is a child and under age, he does not differ from a slave, although he is the master of all the estate; but he is under guardians and

administrators or trustees until the date fixed by his father. So we [Jewish Christians] also, when we were minors, were kept like slaves under [the rules of the Hebrew ritual and subject to] the elementary teachings of a system of external observations and regulations.

Galatians 4:1–3, AMP

According to Roman law, any child who was orphaned was placed under the supervision of a guardian or tutor until the child reached the age of fourteen. Then a trusted manager oversaw the estate until the heir reached the age of 25. At that point, the heir could take over his inheritance.

Also in Roman culture, the children in wealthy families were cared for by slaves. The master of the estate would command the servant, who would in turn command the child. In essence, the status of the child was not much different from that of the servant.

In using this illustration, then, Paul explains how he and his fellow Jews were slaves, or in bondage, to the Law. The Law served as the guardian that disciplined the nation of Israel and prepared it for the coming of Christ. They were being trained in basic, rudimentary principles or elementary teachings—like spiritual ABCs.

But the Law was not God's final revelation; it was preparation for the revelation of Jesus. It is important for a child to learn elemental teachings, but if he never looks past them he will never mature. This was the problem that ensnared the religious legalists of Paul's day. Those who focused only on the Law after the coming of Jesus could not embrace their full inheritance. They chose to remain under the Law rather than move into the freedom of their inheritance as sons.

The Law of Moses could reveal sin and control behavior to a certain extent, but it could not pardon a guilty sinner. In fact, it highlighted the separation between man and

47

God: A fence surrounded the Temple, and a veil blocked the entrance to the holy of holies. The Law could not position anyone as heir to God.

Faith in Jesus changes all that. Paul says: "You are all sons of God through faith in Christ Jesus, for all of you who were baptized into Christ have clothed yourselves with Christ" (Galatians 3:26–27).

When we clothe ourselves with Christ we are laying down the old, dirty garments of sin and putting on robes of righteousness. This analogy of clothing to describe a new spiritual position would have been a familiar one to the new believers of Galatia: When a Roman child came of age, he took off his childhood garments and put on a white woolen garment—a toga—with purple stripes. This garment was cherished as a symbol of adulthood.

Given Equal Status

Not only have believers put on a new garment of adulthood, but Paul shares the astonishing revelation that all are one in Christ. There is no room for exclusivity among believers. "There is neither Jew nor Greek, slave nor free, male nor female, for you are all one in Christ Jesus. If you belong to Christ, then you are Abraham's seed, and heirs according to the promise" (verses 28–29).

The Jews took pride in being God's covenant people; anyone else was considered to be under God's curse. The Greeks, on the other hand, took pride in being culturally privileged; everyone else was classed as barbarian. These distinctions were no longer valid. In Jesus all are heirs according to the promise.

Paul continues to astound his listeners by stating that believers are neither slave nor free, male nor female. In the Galatians' society, slaves were pieces of property. Women were kept confined and disrespected. The Pharisees had their own sense of superiority. As Warren Wiersbe notes in *The Bible Exposition Commentary*: "The Pharisees would pray each morning, 'I thank God, that I am a Jew, not a Gentile; a man, not a woman; and a freeman, and not a slave.' Yet all these distinctions are removed 'in Christ.'"

When it pertains to our spiritual relationship to God through Christ, one's race, sex or political status is not a handicap. In Christ all are positioned on the same level.

God made a promise to Abraham's seed, and that seed was Christ. When we are in Christ, we, too, are Abraham's seed. As such we are recipients of the blessings promised to Abraham's children. Even though we may not be born physically into the nation of Israel, as sons of God we are enriched because of God's promise to Abraham. Our spiritual walk ought to take on a new meaning with the realization of all we have in Christ through grace.

Living as Heirs of God

Now that we understand our position of sonship, we can begin to grasp the fact that we are heirs of God. We have a powerful inheritance, and it is available to us now, not in the future. "Because you are sons, God sent the Spirit of his Son into our hearts, the Spirit who calls out, 'Abba, Father.' So you are no longer a slave, but a son; and since you are a son, God has made you also an heir" (Galatians 4:6–7).

The Greek word for *heir* is *kleronomos*, which means "the recipient of divine promises." Heir is connected with sonship: An heir is one who receives his allotted possessions by right of sonship. This inheritance is linked with the Kingdom. Jesus said: "Therefore I tell you that the kingdom of God will be taken away from you and given to a people who will produce its fruit" (Matthew 21:43).

Jesus spoke these words to the Jews of His day who refused to believe in Him, but the message applies equally to us today. The Kingdom and its power will be taken away from those who fail to remain faithful to Christ by rejecting His righteous ways. It will be given instead to a people who separate themselves from the world and seek first God's Kingdom and righteousness. As we embrace Christ and His righteous ways, we become sons and heirs of God, and our inheritance is the Kingdom.

Not only are we heirs of God, but we are also co-heirs with Christ. All that has been given to Jesus is made available to us: "Now if we are children, then we are heirs—heirs of God and co-heirs with Christ, if indeed we share in his sufferings in order that we may also share in his glory" (Romans 8:17). A co-heir is a fellow receiver. It involves joint participation. We are fellow heirs with Christ and as such are called to participate in extending the Kingdom of God.

Our positions as joint heirs with Christ begin at salvation. All that belongs to Christ as the Firstborn also belongs to us, His brothers and sisters. This includes suffering with Him in this present time, as well as our glory with Him at His return. In order to enter into our rights, we must accept the whole inheritance, suffering as well as glory.

Does this mean the Lord wants us to walk through life as victims and not as victors? Absolutely not. But we will all experience times of struggle, hardship and persecution. We will also experience temptation from the enemy. As we will see in chapter 5, if we want to gain the fullness of our purpose, destiny and calling, if we want to wear the crown, we must also embrace the cross. Jesus is just as concerned with our character as He is with our anointing. We have to die to self daily. But it is in this place of total surrender that we discover true freedom and can then begin to walk in the resurrection power and life of Christ. You see, we must be willing to die, but we must also embrace the resurrection side of the cross.

Those of us in the Western Church do not face the threat of severe persecution for our faith. We are fortunate to live in a nation where we can worship as we choose. But we must be careful that we do not fall into complacency and passivity in our walk of faith or we will lose the freedoms we enjoy. Many brothers and sisters around the world—as many as *two hundred million believers*—suffer for their faith daily. In countries like North Korea, Vietnam, Laos, Iran, China, Egypt, Morocco, Jordan, Iraq, Saudi Arabia, Indonesia —the list goes on—Christians can be imprisoned, tortured or murdered for trusting in the name of Jesus. In some countries, converts to Christianity are killed by their own family members.

Men, women and children around the world pay a high price for their faith, just as Jesus, Peter, Paul and Stephen did. Being a believer does not guarantee that there will not be struggles, hardship, trials, tribulations and persecutions. Just the opposite. Suffering is part of the call of spreading the Good News of the Kingdom of God and discipling the nations.

Access to the Throne

A crown awaits all who die believing in the name of Jesus, but we have seen that we do not have to wait until death to receive our inheritance. Our faith means that through the blood of Christ we, like our great High Priest, have access to the throne room and all the benefits of a kingly inheritance.

The following verse is one of my favorites because it states who we are in Christ: "You are a chosen people, a royal priesthood, a holy nation, a people belonging to God, that you may declare the praises of him who called you out of darkness into his wonderful light" (1 Peter 2:9).

The Greek word for *belonging* is *peripoiesin*. This points to our position as heirs of God and co-heirs with Christ. We are:

- A set-apart nation
- A people consecrated for God's own possession
- A consecrated class of people
- A purchased people
- An acquired people
- A people for purpose
- A people for action

Another Scripture that refers to our walking in light on the earth is this: "[Give] thanks to the Father, who has qualified you to share in the inheritance of the saints in the kingdom of light. For he has rescued us from the dominion of darkness and brought us into the kingdom of the Son he loves" (Colossians 1:12–13).

This inheritance can also be translated "parcel of the lot," and is suggestive of the way in which the Promised Land was given to the Israelites. When they reached Canaan, Joshua cast lots to determine which tribe would receive which parcel of land.

Our inheritance is also attached to land—the Kingdom of light. Our Lord delivered us from the tyrannical dominion of darkness and drew us to Himself—a transference from a skewed, ignorant, dark tyranny and dictatorship to a well-ordered sovereignty. The language used in this Scripture does not depict a casual episode. Jesus, the mighty conqueror, snatched us out of one condition and positioned us in another. We are now part of His Kingdom and under the rulership of the true King.

What a wonderful position! We are poised to receive a powerful inheritance through Jesus and the seal of the Holy Spirit in our lives; we are welcomed as adult sons of God for the purpose of influence in this earth; we are heirs of God and co-heirs with Christ; our inheritance is a territory over which we are called to rule; we are a royal, kingly priesthood of bridge builders who have been created for purpose and action; and we have been blessed with the gift to enter the throne room of God to worship and commune with Him.

Let's see now just what influence we were meant to have—just what were the effects of the Fall?—and begin to understand our mandate to stand in the earth for the Lord.

4

CREATION WAITS
WITH EAGER EXPECTATION

When Adam relinquished his dominion to Satan, creation became slave to corruption. By inviting evil to be at home in the world, Adam led creation into the bondage of sin, corruption and decay. Likewise, when we embrace sinful actions and rebellion, we affect the territory to which we have been called. One of the consequences of our ungodly evil choices is further curse and defilement of land: "The earth dries up and withers, the world languishes and withers. . . . The earth is defiled by its people; they have disobeyed the laws, violated the statutes and broken the everlasting covenant. Therefore a curse consumes the earth" (Isaiah 24:4–6).

Let's recall the directive that God gave man regarding his relationship to creation:

> God spoke: "Let us make human beings in our image, make them reflecting our nature so they can be responsible for the fish in the sea, the birds in the air, the cattle, and, yes, Earth itself, and every animal that moves on the face of Earth." God created human beings; he created them godlike, reflecting God's nature. He created them male and female. God blessed them: "Prosper! Reproduce! Fill Earth! Take charge! Be responsible for fish in the sea and birds in the air, for every living thing that moves on the face of Earth."
>
> Genesis 1:26–28, MESSAGE

It is obvious that this mandate has been, for the most part, unfulfilled. Instead of taking responsible care of the earth as good stewards, ruling the earth with wisdom from God, we continue to sin and to defile the land. Actually, mankind worships the creation instead of subduing it. The concept of "Mother Earth" as an entity to be worshiped or consulted for guidance is one more in a long list of sins against our Creator.

So far we have seen that two cataclysmic events affected the dominion that we were given at creation: Adam sinned and the earth fell prey to corruption; but then Jesus conquered sin and death at the cross. Where does this leave us now in relation to the created world? Let's begin our discussion by investigating another biblical event that affects our current position: the mandate and promise that God gave Noah and the earth following the Flood.

God's Covenant with Noah

From the time of the Fall until Noah, mankind grew increasingly wicked. Men were driven by lust and violence;

harsh words were spoken out against our Father. Sadly, this sounds reminiscent of our culture today. Because of man's evil ways, the Lord was grieved and filled with pain:

> The LORD saw how great man's wickedness on the earth had become, and that every inclination of the thoughts of his heart was only evil all the time. The LORD was grieved that he had made man on the earth, and his heart was filled with pain. So the LORD said, "I will wipe mankind, whom I have created, from the face of the earth—men and animals, and creatures that move along the ground, and birds of the air—for I am grieved that I have made them."
>
> Genesis 6:5–7

Notice God's expression of emotion: His heart was filled with pain. This revelation that God can feel grief and regret makes it clear that He shares a personal, intimate relationship with His creation. He is always about His business, which seems centered on His attentiveness to our condition.

The word *grieved* implies that God's attitude of forbearance and mercy would now express itself in judgment. Even though God's character and ultimate purposes remain changeless, His love and perfection demand that He deal righteously with humans.

Amidst the widespread rebellion on earth, God found one man who still sought communion with Him: "Noah was a righteous man, blameless among the people of his time, and he walked with God" (verse 9). By God's grace Noah did not follow the wicked ways of society but chose to walk rightly with God, which positioned him to receive favor: Noah and his family would be protected from destruction.

> The earth was depraved and putrid in God's sight, and the land was filled with violence (desecration, infringement, out-

rage, assault, and lust for power). And God looked upon the world and saw how degenerate, debased, and vicious it was, for all humanity had corrupted their way upon the earth and lost their true direction. God said to Noah, I intend to make an end of all flesh, for through men the land is filled with violence; and behold, I will destroy them and the land.

verses 11–13, AMP

God told Noah that the land was filled with violence, decay and ruin because of men. Human violence, desecration, sexual lust, lust for power and all other forms of ungodliness had affected the land and led to His judgment. Thus, the wicked people and the land, including most of the animals, would be destroyed. God did not remove the world from existence, obviously, but He did cause destruction of the land and its people through the flood—meaning that He caused the surface of the earth to perish as the dwelling place of man as well as causing all of mankind to perish. Noah and his family were delivered by building and residing in a great ark.

Now we are all familiar with the story of how it rained for forty days and forty nights. The Bible tells us that "all the springs of the great deep burst forth, and the floodgates of the heavens were opened" (Genesis 7:11). Noah and his family and the various pairs of animals were on the ark for 377 days. When the earth was dry, all the living creatures on the ark came out.

The first thing Noah did in the new world was build an altar and worship the Lord. The aroma of the sacrifice was pleasing to the Lord.

Then Noah built an altar to the LORD and, taking some of all the clean animals and clean birds, he sacrificed burnt offerings on it. The LORD smelled the pleasing aroma and said

58

in his heart: "Never again will I curse the ground because of man, even though every inclination of his heart is evil from childhood. And never again will I destroy all living creatures, as I have done. As long as the earth endures, seedtime and harvest, cold and heat, summer and winter, day and night will never cease."

Genesis 8:20–22

After causing His anger to rest upon the world of sinners, the Lord's compassion began to rest on the small remnant of people who remained on the earth. Remember, God loves mankind and desires a relationship with all of His children. He had placed a curse on the ground at the first introduction of sin in the Garden, and He added to the curse with the Flood. But following His judgment, in spite of man's evil thinking and ways, the Lord determined never again to curse the ground or living creatures in this manner.

Here we begin to see the restoration process of the position of mankind in the Garden. Notice in these next verses the reappearance of a familiar mandate:

Then God blessed Noah and his sons, saying to them, "Be fruitful and increase in number and fill the earth. The fear and dread of you will fall upon all the beasts of the earth and all the birds of the air, upon every creature that moves along the ground, and upon all the fish of the sea; they are given into your hands.

Genesis 9:1–2

God spoke to Noah as He had to Adam! The Lord gave Noah, whose name means "a man of the soil," the directive to be fruitful, multiply and increase, and He placed all living creatures under his care, authority and stewardship. Even in Noah's fallen, sinful state, the Lord expressed His desire to partner together in the rule, dominion and stewardship of creation.

The Lord further promised that He would never again cut off all life and destroy the world by a flood. He sealed this mandate with the covenant of the rainbow.

> Then God spoke to Noah and to his sons with him, saying, Behold, I establish My covenant or pledge with you and with your descendants after you and with every living creature that is with you—whether the birds, the livestock, or the wild beasts of the earth along with you, as many as came out of the ark—every animal of the earth. I will establish My covenant or pledge with you: Never again shall all flesh be cut off by the waters of a flood; neither shall there ever again be a flood to destroy the earth and make it corrupt. And God said, This is the token of the covenant (solemn pledge) which I am making between Me and you and every living creature that is with you, for all future generations: I set My bow [rainbow] in the cloud, and it shall be a token or sign of a covenant or solemn pledge between Me and the earth. And it shall be that when I bring clouds over the earth and the bow [rainbow] is seen in the clouds, I will [earnestly] remember My covenant or solemn pledge which is between Me and you and every living creature of all flesh; and the waters will no more become a flood to destroy and make all flesh corrupt. When the bow [rainbow] is in the clouds and I look upon it, I will [earnestly] remember the everlasting covenant or pledge between God and every living creature of all flesh that is upon the earth. And God said to Noah, This [rainbow] is the token or sign of the covenant or solemn pledge which I have established between Me and all flesh upon the earth.
>
> verses 8–17, AMP

God established a new covenant with Noah: Never again would He destroy man and the earth by flood. If Noah and his descendants would honor the Lord's mandate, they would experience His blessing and the earth would respond with fruitfulness.

We know, unfortunately, that it was not long before mankind again fell into uninhibited wickedness. And what was God's response? Centuries later He called forth Abraham and forged a new covenant with him, promising that Abraham's descendants would be as numerous as the stars in the sky, and that in him all families on earth would be blessed.

We see this pattern throughout the Old Testament: The Lord gives revelation concerning a new move of His Spirit regarding the relationship between man and creation and establishes a new covenant. Another example is Joshua. After forty years in the wilderness, a generation grasped the concept of freedom, inheritance and possessing the land. I want to look at his story briefly, because it gives us a picture of land and people at rest.

The Land at Rest

Moses was the deliverer called by God to rescue the nation of Israel from bondage in Egypt. He led the nation from captivity to the land of Canaan that had been promised to Abraham's offspring. During the forty-year wilderness journey, his aide, Joshua, served Moses and the Lord in the Tent of Meeting. He was a young man who knew the presence and voice of the Lord.

As Moses went into the tent, the pillar of cloud would come down and stay at the entrance, while the LORD spoke with Moses. . . . The LORD would speak to Moses face to face, as a man speaks with his friend. Then Moses would return to

the camp, but his young aide Joshua son of Nun did not
leave the tent.

Exodus 33:9, 11

When it came time for the Promised Land to be taken,
it was Joshua who led the nation of Israel to victory. As the
tribes possessed their inheritance, the Lord required them
to drive out all their enemies, all who worshiped idols and
served pagan gods. Every place on which the feet of the Israelites walked, the Lord gave to them. Due to their obedience
and faithfulness to possess the land, the nation of Israel and
the land itself experienced rest.

> So the LORD gave Israel all the land he had sworn to give
> their forefathers, and they took possession of it and settled
> there. The LORD gave them rest on every side, just as he had
> sworn to their forefathers. Not one of their enemies withstood
> them; the LORD handed all their enemies over to them. Not
> one of all the LORD's good promises to the house of Israel
> failed; every one was fulfilled.

Joshua 21:43–45

The nation of Israel experienced victory and rest in the
Promised Land—for as long as Joshua and his generation
were alive. The people did not maintain their faithfulness and
subjected themselves to the effects of the curse once again.

The Lord still had a plan despite man's repeated failure to
walk in covenant with Him. It was Jesus' ministry on earth and
the men and women who partner with Him faithfully that
fulfill His purposes regarding our walking in dominion.

Jesus Liberates Creation

Jesus was the first man to walk the earth since Adam
in complete dominion over creation. We have noted, for

instance, that the seas became calm at His word; the fig tree withered at His rebuke. Not only did He rule, reign and exhibit stewardship during His ministry, but even in His death creation bowed to the true King. The gospel of Matthew gives the picture of the power encounter that took place at Jesus' triumphal sacrifice.

> And Jesus cried again with a loud voice and gave up His spirit. And at once the curtain of the sanctuary of the temple was torn in two from top to bottom; the earth shook and the rocks were split. The tombs were opened and many bodies of the saints who had fallen asleep in death were raised [to life]; and coming out of the tombs after His resurrection, they went into the holy city and appeared to many people. When the centurion and those who were with him keeping watch over Jesus observed the earthquake and all that was happening, they were terribly frightened and filled with awe, and said, Truly this was God's Son!
>
> Matthew 27:50–54, AMP

Creation responded to the establishment of the government of God and the overthrow of Satan's dominion.

When Jesus voluntarily and obediently gave up His Spirit, He cried in a loud voice. This signifies one who was still operating in strength. Usually those who are near death seem to find it difficult to speak, particularly as they release their last breaths on earth. Jesus, however, did not release His Spirit in a weak manner. He called out with a loud voice—perhaps as an announcement not only to those who were witnessing His death, but also to the spiritual realm of Satan and his army of demons. This was a declaration that He had successfully completed the mission of redeeming mankind and creation through the cross.

Redemption for All

The particular time of day and year that Jesus gave up His Spirit coincided with the annual sacrifice of the Passover lamb as the priests made atonement for the sins of the Jews. At that moment, Jesus became the ultimate sacrifice, making atonement for the sins of all mankind. The veil in the Temple was rent in two from top to bottom, making a new way for all people, Jew and Gentile, male or female, free man or slave to enter into the Lord's presence through a personal relationship with Jesus. No longer were animal sacrifices required. They were not necessary because Jesus was the perfect sacrifice given once for all.

The Temple itself was divided into various courts—the holy of holies, the holy place, the priest's court, Israel's court, and courts for women and Gentiles. A dividing wall, approximately three or four feet high, ran through the Temple area separating the court of the Gentiles from the inner court into which only the Jews were permitted. No longer was man's relationship with God dependent on trying to fulfill the Law as determined by the Jewish religious leaders. No longer was there any separation based on the sex, race, ethnicity or political status of those who desired to worship the true King.

Many Raised to Life

The power of death was defeated once and for all at the death and resurrection of Jesus. One of the miraculous signs was the opening of the tombs with many bodies of dead saints coming forth and appearing in the city. Can you imagine the response of those in the city to whom they appeared? It must have been a frightening and awesome experience to witness the power of death being defeated.

Many say that the tombs were opened as a result of the earthquake, which is a highly probable explanation. I find it interesting that the Greek word *anoigo* means "to open," and it refers to God as the one who does the opening. And *egeiro* is the word used for "to be raised, to wake up, arouse or rise from the dead." When the power of death was defeated by Jesus, the ground could not hold the dead. This also serves as the prophetic sign that the redeemed will be raised and with Him upon His return.

The Earth Shook and Rocks Split

Scripture also explains that the earth shook and rocks split. This term for *earth* means "the entire earth, all of the land." This was not limited to Golgotha or even Jerusalem. The entire creation shook. Obviously, this was a violent reaction in response to the blood of our Savior being spilled on the land.

Genesis 4:10 tells us that when Cain killed Abel, the blood of Abel cried out to the Lord from the ground. When the righteous are killed the blood spills on the land and cries out for justice. This was the first instance of blood defiling the land; throughout Scripture we read that death, violence, idolatry, adultery, sexual immorality and broken covenants, among other sins, also defile the land and creation. (In *Authority to Tread* [Chosen, 2005] I explain in depth the open doors that lead to defilement of the land, and how to strategically cleanse the land and break the dark powers of these entry points.)

On a personal level, we understand that the blood of Jesus cleanses, heals, protects, sets free, forgives, releases and breaks the power of death and Satan. It is through the shedding of His blood, His death on the cross and His resurrection that we are redeemed. But the Lord came not only to redeem us and defeat the schemes of Satan in our lives, but also to reclaim, restore and reestablish His rule on the earth. As His blood spilled on the earth and He gave up His Spirit, His blood not only redeemed, healed, delivered and transformed us, it also did the same for the physical creation. It is now our Lord's blood that cries out from the land for the souls of man and all of creation.

The Greek word for *shook* is *seio*. It is translated "to shake, tremble, quake, move in the earth or cause a cosmic disturbance." This word is normally used in the context of God's wrath and judgment. In the scene of the crucifixion, we might think of the earthquake as a manifestation of God's judgment against those who killed Jesus—and that would be true. But there is another meaning as well. *Seio* also denotes "an emotional disturbance through fear, the stirring up or agitation of a crowd and the upsetting of governmental affairs." The whole earth shook as our Savior died. In this shaking was the tearing down, stripping and disarming of the satanic government over creation and the reestablishment of the government of the Kingdom of God.

The Greek word used for *split* is *schizo*. It is translated "to break, chop, cleave, divide, open, rend, separate, split and tear." The rocks split in response to the earthquake, but they also split in response to the tearing down of the power Satan had established in the Garden. The old covenant was fulfilled and, as we will discuss in chapter 8, the new covenant of Jesus as the Rock of revelation upon which the Church stands was established. When a power confrontation in the spiritual realm occurs and defilement is broken off the land, Satan and his army of darkness lose their hold, and the land and the rest of creation respond.

Yet, Creation Waits

Creation was intended to glorify God and for mankind to subdue it. As a result of the sin of Adam and the human race throughout history, it has been subjected instead to bondage. The very environment in which we were created to work has moved into deterioration because of our disobedience. Creation cannot freely glorify the Lord in the condition of oppression. It is, therefore, waiting with eager expectation for the sons of God to take their rightful places. In other words, the land is waiting to be freed from bondage and to be restored into fruitful and peaceful conditions.

Paul explains our relationship with creation and our role of seeing it freed in Romans 8:18–23:

[But what of that?] For I consider that the sufferings of this present time (this present life) are not worth being compared with the glory that is about to be revealed to us and in us and for us and conferred on us! For [even the whole] creation (all nature) waits expectantly and longs earnestly for God's sons to be made known [waits for the revealing, the disclosing of their sonship]. For the creation (nature) was subjected to frailty (to futility, condemned to frustration), not because of some intentional fault on its part, but by the will of Him Who so subjected it—[yet] with the hope that nature (creation) itself will be set free from its bondage to decay and corruption [and gain an entrance] into the glorious freedom of God's children. We know that the whole creation [of irrational creatures] has been moaning together in the pains of labor until now. And not only the creation, but we ourselves too, who have and enjoy the firstfruits of the [Holy] Spirit [a foretaste of the blissful things to come] groan inwardly as we wait for the redemption of our bodies [from sensuality and the grave, which will reveal] our adoption (our manifestation as God's sons).

AMP

The verses given above follow Paul's declaration, given in Romans 8:17, that we are heirs of God and co-heirs of

Christ, which we discussed in chapter 3. Paul states that, as heirs, the sufferings experienced in this present time are not worthy to be compared to the glory that will be made known in us and through us and that will be given to us. We are recipients of a bright and glorious inheritance. We will rule and reign with Jesus throughout our lives and eternity.

It is hard to comprehend the idea that an awesome, powerful and sovereign God has chosen us weak and imperfect beings to partner with Him in this great responsibility. But the truth is, He has chosen to do just that. We have been created for a purpose with spheres of responsibility. This is why it is so crucial for us to embrace the ideas that all good things come from our Father and all good things He has given us are gifts. We have done nothing ourselves or in our own strength.

In the above verses Paul refers to the redemption of our bodies. This means "uncovering" in the sense of making known through revelation or revealing what was not known. In Hebrew this uncovering denotes nakedness or uncovering of all that can be disclosed or revealed. We are not to look at this redemption as a promise only for the future, but one that is playing a role in the timing of the establishment of the new heaven and earth. As stated by Peter: "You ought to live holy and godly lives as you look forward to the day of God and *speed* its coming" (2 Peter 3:11–12, emphasis added).

Our bodies and spiritual position must be seen here and now, therefore, as things that are being raised up. Through the guidance of our Lord and the Holy Spirit, we can be—and should be—a confident, humble, victorious and expectant body of believers who stand on earth for the Lord, spreading the news that the Kingdom of God has come, reaching the lost for Christ and discipling the nations of the world.

We should not look to these verses as an escape clause from responsibility in creation now because of some future redemption that will take place. This is a directive of the Lord that we are to embrace now.

You see, creation is eagerly waiting in earnest expectation and moaning in pains of labor concerning its release from bondage into freedom. The phrase *earnest expectation* is derived from the Greek word *apokaradokia*. This word actually contains three Greek words: *apo* is interpreted as "away"; *kara* means "the head"; and *dokiem* means "to watch." Combined together, the words depict watching with the head erect and outstretched. They suggest waiting in suspense, like a watchman awaiting a beacon or signal to announce a victory in battle.

The Greek word for *moaning* is *sustenazo* and for *pains of labor* is *sunodino*. The two words coupled together signify that the whole creation is united in travail for deliverance from its bondage. The whole world of nature sighs for relief from the agony of the ages, convulsing in birth pangs and awaiting deliverance. It is not the cry of agony as in the throes of death, but of birth. Just as a woman in labor has the hope of birthing her child, so creation also travails in hope and expectancy.

The word *creation* here refers to all of God's creation below the human level that has been enslaved to corruption. And it is called to receive the blessing of freedom and redemption. The good news is, mankind—you and I—are the firstfruits of the changes and blessings that the Spirit has produced in the lives of those redeemed through Jesus. As firstfruits, therefore, we can influence this earth. Kenneth S. Wuest in his *Word Studies from the Greek New Testament* (Eerdmans, 1997) notes that: "Creation is not inert, utterly unspiritual, alien to our life and its hope. What rises from it is the music of humanity."

What a profound statement! Creation plays the music we have composed in this earth realm. What we orchestrate, creation plays as a well-rehearsed orchestra under the guidance of a renowned conductor. If creation can resound with melody in the midst of bondage and corruption due to man's sinful stewardship, then it can also play a newly composed piece of freedom and fruitfulness when we take our rightful places.

How Creation Responds

I would like to share a powerful example of how the creation responds when defilement is broken and the rule of the Kingdom of God is established.

The focus for this particular prayer team was Rainbow Falls, Colorado, which is on the original road to the Ute Pass and is located in Manitou Springs. The Ute Pass was a road used during the gold and silver rush. As a result this location became an entry point for greed and a spirit of mammon. In addition, the spring that feeds the falls was worshiped by the Native Americans; the "Great Spirit of Manitou" was a sacred site to many First Nation tribes.

Making our way down the path toward the waterfall, we sensed that a great deal of bloodshed had occurred in the area; it was as though you could feel death permeating the atmosphere. It was extremely oppressive. Adding to the sense of heaviness was the evidence of disdain for a once-beautiful place of creation: Graffiti was sprawled across the rocks; trash floated in the water; empty beer bottles were flung everywhere; the destitute and homeless hid in hand-crafted shelters. We knew that there was much witchcraft and occult activity in this area.

As we approached the foot of the falls, we came upon a homeless woman sitting on the ground with her choice of liquor in a paper sack placed next to her. She decided to leave as the team passed. We took a moment and prayed for her salvation and deliverance from her bondage to alcohol.

Just as we reached the foot of the falls, team members began to speak revelation as the Lord directed. It was very evident that the Lord sent us there to war against the strongholds the enemy had established. The Lord spoke clearly that this was a "spiritual vortex," or open door allowing a current of demonic activity into the region. A prophetic word came forth revealing that rape, abortion and other deaths had occurred on the land. We also had a sense that pregnant women had been torn open.

The Lord revealed to us that there were spiritual ties to Egypt, and that the bloodshed on the ground was committed by Freemasons. General Chivington was one of the early leaders of Manitou Springs, and he was a Mason. He was also responsible for the famous Sand Creek Indian Massacre, which occurred in the state of Colorado. We broke the power of death from General Chivington and Freemasonry from the location, along with all ties to Egypt. We severed the tie of death between Rainbow Falls and Sand Creek. We also dealt with the spirit of Leviathan and all demonic powers in the water flowing from this place of death into Manitou Springs. The local pastor who was praying with us drove a stake into the ground declaring the land cleansed. He then did the same in the water. He declared the demonic spiritual vortex closed over Manitou. It was very intense and very strategic.

As this was completed, we entered a powerful time of worship. We then released a "shout of the Lord" over the land and the water. The prophetic declaration was given that the water would be cleansed and no longer contaminated and that the land would be cleansed of all defilement. We spoke to the land to bring forth life.

Just two days after we cleaned the "vortex" spiritually, it was cleaned physically, as reported in the local newspaper, *The Gazette*, in an article by R. Scott Rappold. The pastor from Manitou Springs who prayed with us said he had never before heard anyone outside his church refer to Rainbow Falls as a vortex.

They used to call this place Rainbow Falls.

It was sacred to the Ute Indians. The first road up the pass to the gold fields beyond went through it. Some of the more metaphysical Manitou Springs residents believe it is a "spiritual vortex."

These days, though, it's known sardonically as "graffiti falls."

"The first time I came up here, I was like, 'Am I at the right place? This is gross,'" said L'Aura Montgomery Rutt, who moved to Manitou Springs from Pennsylvania and heard about the waterfall.

She was shocked by the trash-strewn paths, the beer bottles along the creek, the paint cans floating in the water, the graffiti that adorns the rocks. So she decided to clean up this unknown wedge of land west of Manitou Springs, which has one of the most spectacular waterfalls in the area.

About 20 volunteers joined her Saturday, for what they hope was the first of many days to restore this hidden glen—with a 20-foot waterfall and swimming hole—to its former beauty.

"It's just a huge eyesore. Every time I drive by, it bugs me. And no one's doing anything about it," Lane Williams said between spraying rocks with a power washer.

Though once a popular tourist destination, Rainbow Falls sank into obscurity after the state built the bulky bridge to U.S. Highway 24 over it. Dirt was piled up on the old shelf road leading to it, and, since it is outside of the Manitou Springs city limits in unincorporated El Paso County, nobody took responsibility to maintain it.

"This is one of the most beautiful places in the Manitou area and it's one of the most neglected," said Mike Maio, with a trash bag full of refuse he collected from the banks of Fountain Creek.

Organizers approached the Manitou Springs government about cleaning it, and were told it was out of their jurisdiction—though the city did lend a water truck for the occasion. United Rentals Inc. provided the power washer and Savelli's Pizza donated food for volunteers.

It became quickly apparent that picking up the trash was the easy part. Removing the graffiti proved more difficult.

They wanted to do it without chemicals, but the power washer did little to strip the paint from the rocks.

"It's really not going to make a huge impact when we're done, but hopefully we'll generate enough guilt in the county they'll come up with their big equipment," said Williams, taking a break from the painstaking power-washing.

Rutt envisions it becoming a county park some day. But for now, about the only time it gets any official attention is when rescue crews have to pluck a teenager from the rocks.

Organizers plan more clean-up days, and hoped to get a sand-blaster or other equipment for removing the paint next time.

While she gingerly picked up pieces of broken glass from the mud, volunteer Katherine Garcia said it could be one of the area's nicest parks.

"It's beautiful if you go far enough down to see the falls and it's worth keeping it nice," she said. "It's the biggest falls I've seen here."

What an awesome God we serve! Friend, when we stand in the territory the Lord calls us to, change will begin to manifest in the earth. Let's investigate further the promise of our inheritance in regard to creation.

The Meek Shall Inherit the Earth

Not only does God desire for us to preach the message of the Kingdom and to build up and edify His Church, but He also wants us to stand on the earth for Him. Creation will not be free until His people obediently rise up to reconcile it.

Jesus said that the meek shall inherit the earth. Now, being meek does not mean being a pushover. Jesus was angry with those who were making the Temple a place to sell their goods. He overturned their tables and benches and would not allow anyone to carry merchandise through the Temple courts and accused them of making it a den of robbers (see Mark 11:15–17). Moses was humble—in fact, he is called the meekest man on earth (see Numbers 12:3)—but he stood up to Pharaoh on behalf of the nation of Israel and performed miraculous signs and wonders. When required, they were bold and forthright in the anointing of the Holy Spirit. We must not mistake meekness for lack of passion, authority or power. Meekness is the condition of gentleness, humility coupled with a bold faith and total obedience to the Lord.

As we live meek lives of submission to the Lord, the promise is the inheritance of the earth. The word *earth* can also be translated *land*. It means we are given a portion of property as a possession. I want to share a powerful model of this kind of meekness and the miraculous, transforming result it has had on man and creation. The following story was written by Sarah Pollak.

Imagine a town where there are so few crimes, the jails have closed, the crops are so big and luscious—they could have come from the Garden of Eden.

This is happening in a small town in Guatemala where spiritual revival led to a remarkable transformation.

There's a small town nestled high in the western mountains of Guatemala called Almolonga. Here, economic conditions are proving a remarkable exception to the national norm.

The majority of Almolonga's 18,000 residents are farmers. Much of the work is still done by hand, including cultivation and irrigation. What sets Almolonga apart from other farming villages in Guatemala is the incredible volume of its agricultural production.

On a typical market day, during one of the eight annual harvests, tons of fresh vegetables are gathered in the town center for export. There they are loaded onto large tractor-trailers. About 40 trucks a day leave Almolonga, loaded down with some of the finest produce grown in the western hemisphere. It is no wonder that this village is called "America's Vegetable Patch."

But there is something else that distinguishes Almolonga besides its vegetables. And it is also something villagers like to speak about on signs leading into town: "Jesus is Lord of Almolonga." And that has made all the difference.

Juan Riscajche is a typical Almolongan farmer. His strong Christian faith is as real to him as the vegetables he lovingly tends by hand. "Definitely it is a blessing directly from God," Juan explained, "because we know

75

that He is the owner of the whole earth. And he also is the one who provides us with the seed. So the only thing we do is follow His instructions, and you can see the results we have."

His son, Mariano Riscajche, pastors one of the town's largest congregations, "El Calvario" or "Calvary Church."

Mariano vividly remembers the day that God first got his attention. "It was in 1974, I was a real drunk, walking the streets," he recalls. "Then I heard a voice, 'Mariano!' the first time, 'Mariano!' the second time, and the third time, 'Mariano, I've chosen you to come with Me!'"

Mariano was one of the first in a wave of supernatural conversions that swept through Almolonga in the 1970s. A call to repentance and holiness was followed by a period of intense spiritual warfare. He told us about one particular incident, when he felt led to cast a demon out of a drunken man.

"And suddenly from that man's throat came a hoarse voice saying 'No! No! This is mine and you cannot take it away from me. I am powerful and all this town is my domain and nobody can come and intrude in here!'" Mariano said.

The demon told the pastor that his name was "Maximon." Effigies of Maximon have long been venerated in Guatemala, like this one we found in the neighboring village of Zunil. Candles are burned and hard liquor and cigarettes are sacrificed to the idol, who's said to be a combination of Judas Iscariot, Conquistador Pedros Alvarado, and the Mayan deity "Ry Laj Man."

Mariano knew exactly who he was dealing with—and how to respond.

So Mariano said, "'Be quiet! The time has come to take authority over you and this town. At this moment, the Spirit of God is over me! Loose him!' And instantly the man was free!"

And the town became free. It has been estimated that over 90 percent of the Almolongan people are now born-again Christians. A generation ago, there were only four churches here. Today there are 23. The last jail closed down in 1988. There is virtually no crime in this town. The usual form of address is "hermano," or "brother."

Where once there was rampant alcoholism, bars have been closed, or torn down and rebuilt into church halls. The lot where Calvary Church was built was formerly occupied by Almolonga's largest saloon.

Everywhere you look, blessing and prosperity are evident. People who used to pinch centavos to buy a donkey are now driving Toyota pickups. And the trailers that haul away vegetables are most often powered by Mercedes Benz trucks.

Pastor Harold Cabelleros of El Shaddai Church in Guatemala City says repentance and revival have completely transformed Almolonga.

"The mentality and the way of thinking and the patterns of thinking of the people has changed so drastically," Harold said. "Changed from a culture of death, a culture of alcoholism, idolatry, and witchcraft, to a culture today where they think only about expanding the kingdom of God—prosperity, blessing, healing—and everything related to revival."

Mariano says that the miracle of Almolonga should not be unique at all. "Just as God did it here, it can happen everywhere in the world," Mariano says. "What the Lord wants to do, in any place, is to show that, through His power, He can lead people to a better life."

The citizens of Almolonga and the land have experienced a miraculous deliverance—freedom from the dominion of sin and darkness into a life of victory, provision and abundance. In essence, the people of the city embraced the land and treated it with love and affection. It is a "relationship" that echoes the promise of the Lord concerning Zion, Jerusalem and the Church:

> For Zion's sake will I [Isaiah] not hold my peace, and for Jerusalem's sake I will not rest until her imputed righteousness and vindication go forth as brightness, and her salvation radiates as does a burning torch. And the nations shall see your righteousness and vindication [your rightness and justice—not your own, but His ascribed to you], and all kings shall behold your salvation and glory; and you shall be called by a new name which the mouth of the Lord shall name. You shall also be [so beautiful and prosperous as to be thought of as] a crown of glory and honor in the hand of the Lord, and a royal diadem [exceedingly beautiful] in the hand of your God. You [Judah] shall no more be termed Forsaken, nor shall your land be called Desolate any more. But you shall be called Hephzibah [My delight is in her], and your land be called Beulah [married]; for the Lord delights in you, and your land shall be married [owned and protected by the Lord]. For as a young man marries a virgin [O Jerusalem], so shall your sons marry you; and as the bridegroom rejoices over the bride, so shall your God rejoice over you.
>
> Isaiah 62:1–5, AMP

Jesus has promised that the land of Jerusalem will no longer be forsaken or desolate but a place of delight and marriage. Marriage is a binding covenant. When the city and its inhabitants are correctly aligned with God, the land will be owned and protected and therefore will prosper.

Yes, this Scripture is a prophecy speaking of a day when Jerusalem will be filled with the glory and righteousness of God. But, the truth is, when the inhabitants of the land no longer neglect it, but champion it and delight in it as when a man marries a virgin, the land will begin to produce. It releases promises of inheritance and security to a land when its natives and inhabitants stand for the Lord and His righteousness in it, steward it, are pleased with it, prefer it before other lands and resolve to take their lot with it. Almolonga is experiencing just such a covenant blessing with the Lord. And as the people there profess, "Just as God did it here, it can happen everywhere in the world."

Moving Forward

What a powerful message of revival and transformation! Our God is truly an awesome God who desires a people and a land of His own. Beloved, this also applies to you and me. How we should long for the transforming power of our almighty, sovereign God! And not just in our personal lives, but also in our families, neighborhoods, cities, states and nations. Creation is waiting for freedom.

Now, let's move ahead and learn how to apply this freedom to our personal lives, which positions us to influence the territories that we have been assigned by God.

5

Establishing Personal Dominion

For too long we have embraced the mindset of victims in a fallen world. We live as those who are still under a curse instead of walking in the liberty and freedom of the King. There has to be a shift in our spiritual understanding of who we are in Christ and our position in Him. Now, it is true that we are all born with a fallen nature; we all do and will sin. Still, we need to shift our thinking from captive to conqueror, from survivor to victor.

Scripture tells us that we have been given everything that pertains to life and godliness. God has made available to each of us all that is necessary to obtain a life set apart for His worship and service. We do not, however, obtain this condition by osmosis. Paul gives us direction:

Therefore, my dear ones, as you have always obeyed [my suggestions], so now, not only [with the enthusiasm you would show] in my presence but much more because I am absent, work out (cultivate, carry out to the goal, and fully complete) your own salvation with reverence and awe and trembling (self-distrust, with serious caution, tenderness of conscience, watchfulness against temptation, timidly shrinking from whatever might offend God and discredit the name of Christ).

Philippians 2:12, AMP

The spiritual walk always is a process, and it always involves discipline. Even when God moves suddenly in our lives, taking us to a higher plane, we need to develop the obedience that that new place requires. In the amazing story of Almolonga, Guatemala, in the last chapter, for instance, the people have been fervent to respond to God's blessings with increased prayer, spiritual warfare, deliverance and obedience—praising Him for even greater revival and transformation to come. In this sense we play an active part in our spiritual well-being. The issues and problems we face will not disappear until we embrace our destiny with authority and dominion. And the process then must become a lifestyle for the victory to be maintained. In other words, we have to cultivate our relationship with the Lord in order to work out our salvation to its end.

In this chapter we will discuss eight steps for growing in personal dominion.

1. Stop Sinning

One of the first steps toward establishing dominion is to turn from the old self to the new:

Strip yourselves of your former nature [put off and discard your old unrenewed self] which characterized your previous manner of life and becomes corrupt through lusts and desires that spring from delusion; and be constantly renewed in the spirit of your mind [having a fresh mental and spiritual attitude], and put on the new nature (the regenerate self) created in God's image, [Godlike] in true righteousness and holiness.

Ephesians 4:22–24, AMP

In order to walk in personal dominion, we have to lay down the old self, strip off the sin nature, disarm its evil lusts and desires and embrace the new nature of Christlikeness. Even with a sin nature we can gain victory over sinful patterns and walk in righteousness and holiness in this life. I believe it is possible for Christians to reach a place of holiness in which we can walk for some time without sin. As we seek the Lord daily and ask Him to keep us from temptation, the Holy Spirit works in and through us to aid us in our walks.

When we sin, and perhaps especially when we succumb to a repeated pattern of sin, then we are giving the enemy access to our personal lives and territories. In Ephesians 4:27 Paul instructs us to "leave no [such] room or foothold for the devil [give no opportunity to him]" (AMP). The Greek word for *foothold* is *topos*. It is translated "place, location, region, room, opportunity." It implies a geographical region or specific site. When we sin we are giving the devil an opportunity to invade our lives as well as our places, locations and areas of influence and to establish his grip of bondage. In order to have victory, we have to let go of the old sinful patterns and embrace the new nature through Christ.

2. Embrace the Father's Love

Countless individuals forfeit a life of dominion because they are unable to relate to the love of God the Father. Sadly, many endured negative experiences with their earthly fathers and mothers. Some grew up with no affection or "absentee" parents. Others had emotionally and verbally abusive parents, physically abusive parents, addicted parents, sexually abusive parents, controlling parents, etc. Not only is this a sad picture of a fallen world, but it explains why fear and apprehension often carry over to other relationships—even the relationship with a heavenly Father who lavishes nothing but love on us. The ones who have experienced this earthly pain cannot welcome the concept of being sons and daughters of God; rather, they feel orphaned and separate from their kingly inheritance.

God loves us more than we can fathom. He so loves us that He created each of us in His image and likeness in order to have personal relationships with us. He gave His only Son to die on the cross to make atonement for our sins so that we could be set free from the dominion of sin and darkness. He welcomes us as His children and heirs to His Kingdom. We will spend eternity with the desire only to worship and adore Him.

John, the beloved apostle, puts it this way: "How great is the love the Father has lavished on us, that we should be called children of God! And that is what we are! The reason the world does not know us is that it did not know him" (1 John 3:1). The word for *love* is *agape*, and it refers to an abundance of love—a love feast. It is an extravagant love that is without end. It captures God's deepest nature; He is love.

If you are reading this and feel as if you are unable to receive this love because of past hurts, then please consider contacting a ministry that can help you receive deliverance and inner healing. It is time to move out of the prison of victimization and into the freedom of the extravagant love of the Father. This is an important part of walking in personal dominion—submitting yourself for prayer, deliverance and inner healing on issues where you are unable to achieve victory on your own.

Begin to seek the Lord, worship Him and ask Him to touch and reveal more of Himself to you. Place yourself in an atmosphere to receive more of Him by getting connected with a group that is experiencing the manifest presence of the Lord. Ask Him to take you deeper in His presence. Worship Him in spirit and in truth and press into a relationship to know Him more. He is a faithful God.

3. Love Others

As we embrace the love of our Father and grow in confidence, this love will then flow over into our relationships with others.

Love is the governing principle for everyone who wants to rule with Christ. You and I can be operating in great power and seeing awesome miracles occur, but if we do not have love then we are nothing and we gain nothing. We should earnestly desire to walk in the Spirit so that we can help, comfort and bless others. Paul tells us this in his consummate teaching on love:

> If I speak in the tongues of men and of angels, but have not love, I am only a resounding gong or a clanging cymbal. If I have the gift of prophecy and can fathom all mysteries and all knowledge, and if I have a faith that can move mountains, but have not love, I am nothing. If I give all I possess to the poor and surrender my body to the flames, but have not love, I gain nothing. Love is patient, love is kind. It does not envy, it does not boast, it is not proud. It is not rude, it is not self-seeking, it is not easily angered, it keeps no record of wrongs. Love does not delight in evil but rejoices with

the truth. It always protects, always trusts, always hopes, always perseveres.

1 Corinthians 13:1–7

Every aspect of our walk with the Lord is based on relationship—either with Him or His Body on earth. We could make the argument from these verses that a believer who lacks love is in a lost spiritual condition—meaning that it is possible that no true conversion experience has occurred.

Jesus longs for us to be one in the Spirit; He prayed that we would seek unity:

> "My prayer is not for them alone. I pray also for those who will believe in me through their message, that all of them may be one, Father, just as you are in me and I am in you. May they also be in us so that the world may believe that you have sent me. I have given them the glory that you gave me, that they may be one as we are one: I in them and you in me. May they be brought to complete unity to let the world know that you sent me and have loved them even as you have loved me."
>
> John 17:20–23

Our heavenly Father is loving, merciful and gracious toward all of His children. We have done nothing to deserve this love. He asks us to share it with the rest of the Body.

4. Forgive Others

The Father also asks us to forgive. He faithfully extends forgiveness, releasing each of us from our debt of sin, and He expects us in return to forgive those who have offended us. We know from the "love chapter" that we are not to wait for an apology from the offender or keep a checklist of his or her wrongs. The choice to forgive is made without any expectation of an apology or repayment. Forgiveness is a lifestyle choice.

Jesus said this: "If you forgive men when they sin against you, your heavenly Father will also forgive you. But if you do not forgive men their sins, your Father will not forgive your sins" (Matthew 6:14–15). Christians must be ready and willing to forgive the offenses of others. If we do not forgive, then our heavenly Father will not forgive our sins.

Think about this. As Jesus hung on the cross, He cried out, "Father, forgive them, for they do not know what they are doing" (Luke 23:34). Jesus did not wait for an apology from those who were taking His life. As His followers, we should mirror His example.

I remember well a time when I was deeply offended by an issue of betrayal. It did not take long for me to harbor thoughts of bitterness. But soon I realized that even though I was "in the right," I was the loser: I sensed a "wall" growing between myself and the Lord. When I finally acknowledged that I was holding on to unforgiveness, I made the decision to confess that sin and to repent. I released all the hurt to Him and asked Him to help me love with His love the individuals who had so angered me.

He was faithful to answer this prayer: My heart was supernaturally flooded with love and compassion for them. Because of His mercy, my obedience could bear fruit: To this day I truly enjoy time spent with them. Bitterness did not take root in my heart.

I now understand the power of blessing those who persecute us. When hurtful situations develop, our response is critical. Choosing to forgive helps establish personal dominion because it produces the character of Christ in us.

Forgiveness also breaks the back of the enemy. I have learned in my Christian walk that the Lord is able to fight my battles far more successfully than I am. He is in the business of restoration. If God is for us, who can be against us?

5. Grow in Authority through Submission

One of the basic tenets of growing in personal dominion is submission to authority. We will not have true freedom without it. This includes submitting one to another in our marriages and homes, submitting to employers in the workplace in a Christlike manner, submitting to those who are in spiritual authority, submitting to the governing authorities and submitting to the Word of God and to the Lord Himself. If there is no submission, then there will be no authority.

Jesus learned obedience through suffering and overcoming. He learned obedience to the extent that He willingly gave His life—and He did it without murmuring, complaining or embracing a victim mentality. The same is to be true for us. In order to walk in submission, we have to walk in obedience to the Father, His Word and all His ways. Jesus' obedience was for the sake of the Kingdom of God; ours is the same.

Let's discuss briefly the main areas in which we are to operate in submission in order to walk in personal dominion.

In Our Homes

Our homes should exemplify the love of the Lord. Husbands and wives are to submit to one another in love.

Wives, understand and support your husbands in ways that show your support for Christ. The husband provides leadership to his wife the way Christ does to his church, not by domineering but by cherishing. So just as the church submits to Christ as he exercises such leadership, wives should likewise submit to their husbands.

Ephesians 5:22–24, MESSAGE

In writing this verse Paul was referring to the spiritual union between a husband and wife by comparing it to the relationship, communion and spiritual union between Christ and the Church. Actually, in ancient writings the Greek word used here for *leader* or *head* is *kephale*, which many Bible scholars translate as *source*—in the way that the head of a river is its source. This suggests that Adam was the source from which Eve was created.

The husband/wife connection does not mean dictatorship, but loving relationship. Christ so loved the Church that He gave Himself up for her. So the love of a husband should exhibit the willingness to cherish and sacrifice for his wife and family. The wife should partner together with her husband to serve and lead as the Lord directs in their relationship. Marriages are a team, a partnership and love relationship in which the Lord is worshiped and His Kingdom plans furthered.

Children are to submit to their parents as they are brought up in the training and instruction of the Lord. And even when children are older they are to show honor and respect to their parents. "Children, do what your parents tell you. This is only right. 'Honor your father and mother' is the first commandment that has a promise attached to it, namely, 'so you will live well and have a long life'" (Ephesians 6:1–3, MESSAGE). Of the Ten Commandments, this is the first with a special promise, meaning if it is obeyed then there is a blessing from the Lord for a long and good life.

89

At the same time the Lord gives direction to fathers: "Fathers, don't exasperate your children by coming down hard on them. Take them by the hand and lead them in the way of the Master" (verse 4, MESSAGE).

Fathers and mothers are to train the children in the way they are to go. The authority of a parent should never be used to demean, belittle, abuse or unnecessarily control or dominate. Parents are to love the Lord and all His ways and are to model this in the home. As a result, the hearts of the parents must be turned to the hearts of their children, which then draws the heart of the children to the Savior.

Malachi prophesies a powerful word in preparation for the ministry of John the Baptist:

> "See, I will send you the prophet Elijah before that great and dreadful day of the LORD comes. He will turn the hearts of the fathers to their children, and the hearts of the children to their fathers; or else I will come and strike the land with a curse."
>
> Malachi 4:5–6

John the Baptist was the one sent before the Lord to put families right with each other and God, and to lead the disobedient to the wisdom of the righteous (see Luke 1:17). The purity and righteousness of the home was a primary focus on the Lord's heart in establishing the ministry of Jesus. If the fathers' hearts and children's hearts were not turned to one another, the result would have been a curse on the land.

In the Workplace

In the workplace and in the world, we are to set the example:

Stay calm; mind your own business; do your own job. You've heard all this from us before, but a reminder never hurts. We want you living in a way that will command the respect of outsiders, not lying around sponging off your friends.

1 Thessalonians 4:11–12, MESSAGE

Servants, do what you're told by your earthly masters. And don't just do the minimum that will get you by. Do your best. Work from the heart for your real Master, for God, confident that you'll get paid in full when you come into your inheritance. Keep in mind always that the ultimate Master you're serving is Christ. The sullen servant who does shoddy work will be held responsible. Being a follower of Jesus doesn't cover up bad work.

Colossians 3:22–24, MESSAGE

As Christians we are exhorted to do our labor as service to the Lord. We are to work as though Christ is our employer, knowing that all work will be rewarded by Him.

Submission involves not only an act of the will but also an attitude of the heart. Suppose your boss asks you to do a task. You complete the job, but in your heart lurks grumbling, anger, murmuring or resentment. In that case you were obedient but not submissive because your heart was full of cloaked feelings of rebellion. The attitude of our hearts must match the outward performance of the task. Responding in humility and with a Christlike attitude of joy is what it means to submit to an employer.

In Relation to Spiritual Authorities

God places people over us in spiritual authority in order to help us grow and become all the Lord desires us to be. We see examples of this throughout Scripture—relationships of both

91

friendship and spiritual accountability: Elijah and Elisha, Paul and Timothy, Moses and Joshua, Jesus and the disciples—to name just a few. In these relationships, life experiences were the backdrop for spiritual impartation and instruction. The student learned from the teacher and carried the anointing into the next generation.

Here is an important principle: In order to be in authority, we have to be under authority. In order to grow, we have to be taught. This means we bless those in our churches who are leaders. We learn from those who are placed over us. We connect ourselves in spiritual accountability to a person or group of believers—such as a pastor, Bible teacher, ministry leader, Christian friend or home group—who will guide and direct us with wisdom from the Lord. In the Kingdom of God there should be no lone wolves; everyone should have some form of spiritual guidance and accountability. Through these relationships spiritual growth, freedom and maturity will develop—and will result in your own spiritual promotion so that you can help and guide others.

Again, realize that spiritual accountability does not mean control. Accountability relationships guide, instruct, impart love and, when necessary, correct.

In Relation to Governing Authorities

During His ministry on earth, Jesus submitted to all proper authority. When it came time to pay the Temple tax, for instance, He sent Peter to the lake to throw in his line to catch a fish. When Peter opened the mouth of this fish, he found a four-drachma coin, which was enough to pay for Jesus' and Peter's taxes. When asked about paying civil taxes, He said, "Pay therefore to Caesar the things that are due to Caesar, and pay to God the things that are due to God" (Matthew 22:21, AMP). Even though Caesar was a worldly, rebellious man, he held an authoritative position and should be obeyed.

In modern terms, we need to submit to governing laws and those in position of authority, like judges or policemen. Through our obedience to legitimate authority, the Kingdom of God will be extended.

In Relation to the Word of God

The writer of Hebrews gives us amazing insight into the Word of God. Think about these words for a moment:

> The Word that God speaks is alive and full of power [making it active, operative, energizing, and effective]; it is sharper than any two-edged sword, penetrating to the dividing line of the breath of life (soul) and [the immortal] spirit, and of joints and marrow [of the deepest parts of our nature], exposing and sifting and analyzing and judging the very thoughts and purposes of the heart.
>
> Hebrews 4:12, AMP

The Word of God is alive, powerful and active. It is as a double-edged sword that reaches down into all parts of who we are and passes verdict on what is uncovered. It penetrates to the secrets concealed in the innermost cores of our beings where secrets are kept not only from other people but from our own consciousness. It brings to light issues we are unaware of. The Word of God is the greatest source of accountability in our lives.

In Relation to the Lord Himself

Friend, whenever we encounter authority we meet God. We must submit to Him and all His ways. We must love Him, love others, spend time in prayer, spend time in worship, spend time in the Word and take delight in the Lord. Psalm 37:4–9 is a powerful Scripture, full of blessings for those who submit to His ways:

> Delight yourself also in the Lord, and He will give you the desires and secret petitions of your heart. Commit your way to the Lord [roll and repose each care of your load on Him]; trust (lean on, rely on, and be confident) also in Him and He will bring it to pass. And He will make your uprightness and right standing with God go forth as the light, and your justice and right as [the shining sun of] the noonday. Be still and rest in the Lord; wait for Him and patiently lean yourself upon Him; fret not yourself because of him who prospers in his way, because of the man who brings wicked devices to pass. Cease from anger and forsake wrath; fret not yourself—it tends only to evildoing. For evildoers shall be cut off, but those who wait and hope and look for the Lord [in the end] shall inherit the earth.

AMP

If we are faithful to God, He will be faithful to us. When we submit to Him and commit our ways to Him, the enemy will flee. Those who love the Lord and follow Him will receive salvation, freedom, the desires of their hearts, promotion and vindication—and they will inherit the land.

6. Grow into Leadership

I have touched briefly on a point that I want to develop a little more fully. As I travel in ministry, I meet many people who have the same question: "How did you get to a place of leadership? What did God do in your life to allow you promotion?" I know that their hearts are seeking just what mine was seeking when the Lord started me on this path: I felt that there was a calling on my life, but I did not fully understand it. In fact, like these dear ones, I was not looking specifically for leadership: I had a driving desire to know the Lord intimately, to be involved in what He was doing and to serve in any capacity that I could. I just wanted to be where I saw the Lord moving.

And the path He put me on is still unfolding before me. Just about the time I think I have it figured out, the Lord speaks and my direction changes!

But the step for growing in personal dominion is this: In order to lead you have to serve, and yet the motive for serving cannot be leadership. The Lord will be quick to point out the moment that this faulty motive slips into your heart. It never fails that as soon as I begin to think that I have "arrived" and am ready for leadership—or as we say in Texas, the moment that I get too big for my britches—He uses people or situations to bring me into a place of humility.

God is the one who promotes, not man, and He usually takes us through a process of being purified, a process that operates primarily in an atmosphere of service and submission. Look at Jesus' words to His disciples when the mother of James and John asked if her sons could sit with Jesus in His Kingdom, one on the right hand and one on the left:

> When the ten others heard about this, they lost their tempers, thoroughly disgusted with the two brothers. So Jesus got them together to settle things down. He said, "You've observed how godless rulers throw their weight around, how quickly a little power goes to their heads. It's not going to be that way with you. Whoever wants to be great must become a servant. Whoever wants to be first among you must be your slave. That is what the Son of Man has done: He came to serve, not be served—and then to give away his life in exchange for the many who are held hostage."
>
> Matthew 20:24–28, MESSAGE

Now James and John had walked with the Lord, learned from Him, fellowshipped with Him, fed the crowds, traveled from city to city and done many other things that made them feel entitled to receive an affirmative answer to this request. Jesus points out how easy it is for a little power to go to one's head. The true leader, He explains, does not focus on power but on compassion, love and brokenness over a hurting world. Whoever wants to be great, therefore, must become a servant.

I want to mention here that the other side of the leadership coin is spiritual laziness, a condition in which we neglect to follow our Savior into the position He desires for us to have. The writer of Hebrews addresses some who have fallen into just this condition:

> We have much to say about this, but it is hard to explain because you are slow to learn. In fact, though by this time you ought to be teachers, you need someone to teach you the elementary truths of God's word all over again. You need milk, not solid food! Anyone who lives on milk, being still an infant, is not acquainted with the teaching about righteousness. But solid food is for the mature, who by constant use have trained themselves to distinguish good from evil.
>
> Hebrews 5:11–14

Laziness can prevent us from realizing our inheritance and victory, and can dull our ability to hear God's voice. Laziness will cripple any plans of positioning ourselves for freedom and victory. We are to keep our senses clear by staying in the presence of the Lord, reading the Word and focusing on worship. This personal discipline is where our ability to hear and receive instruction from the Lord increases.

7. Watch Out for Fear and Unbelief

Faith is a vital ingredient for establishing personal dominion, yet so many of us are bound by fear and unbelief. Paul likens fear to slavery: "For you did not receive a spirit that makes you a slave again to fear, but you received the Spirit of sonship. And by him we cry, 'Abba, Father'" (Romans 8:15). Proverbs calls it a snare: "Fear of man will prove to be a snare, but whoever trusts in the LORD is kept safe" (Proverbs 29:25). We have all experienced fear in the face of danger, evil or pain. In its most terrifying expression it can be paralyzing. Fear can make us feel unworthy and afraid to welcome the fullness of all that God has for us.

Unbelief is tantamount to distrust. If we embrace unbelief we are telling the Lord that we do not trust His goodness and faithfulness or His promises. Basically, unbelief says, "God, Your promises are true for everybody else, but they do not apply to me." Or the attitude can be one of pride: "I have all the answers I need; I do not need God." Both positions are dangerous. Fear and unbelief cripple us from ever achieving victory or advancing the Kingdom of God.

Let me share a personal story from my life in which I had to obtain freedom from the depths of fear and unbelief.

I accepted Jesus as my Savior when I was twelve years old, and I walked with Him for many years. But there was a time in my adult years when I walked in complete rebellion to all I had been raised to believe. This lasted for three years, a period in my life of which I am not proud. Thank God for praying parents, grandparents and friends! Their prayers caused me to turn from this sin and rebellion back to the Lord.

But my battle was not over. Even though I repented and committed my life back to the Lord, a nagging voice spoke

97

continuously with words of fear, doubt and unbelief concerning my spiritual position of salvation. There was still an open door for the enemy to harass and oppress me.

This harassment went on for several years; I could not shake it. I heard a constant tormenting lie that I was not really a believer because of the sin I had indulged in for those three years. "You just think you are saved," the voice said, "but you are not. You can never have the assurance of salvation. You are unworthy."

Because I allowed fear to live in my heart, I was not able to believe that the power of Jesus Christ was strong enough to save me. I finally fell into depression from the overwhelming belief of unworthiness. There were days I did not feel I had the strength or the desire to get out of bed. The only thing that kept me functioning was my responsibility for our two-year-old daughter.

One day as she was napping, I reached a place of such torment that I fell to the living room floor in tears. "Lord," I said, "I am grabbing hold of the hem of Your garment and setting my face like flint until I get a breakthrough from this torment. God, I choose to trust You."

In a few moments I heard my daughter call for me. I took her into the kitchen and fixed her lunch. I sat next to her at the table as I always did while she ate. I tried with all my strength to appear as the happy mother, but I knew I was failing.

As my daughter ate, her gaze shifted from her food and focused on something in the backyard. She then began to swing her legs in the booster chair and turned to me excitedly. "Mommy," she said, "it is so funny. Mommy, it is so funny."

"Honey, what is so funny?"

Pointing to the backyard with a bright smile on her face, she said, "Out there, Mommy." She then climbed out of her booster chair and began to walk back and forth in front of me like a tiny soldier guarding his post. She then turned and said, "Mommy, it is an angel and Jesus. They are here for you."

I instantly began to weep and thank the Lord for His protecting presence.

That night I determined to receive prayer at church. The Lord and His angels were warring on my behalf, and it was time I did as well. As the evening prayer time ended, I ran to the front and asked one of my closest friends, who was also our home group pastor, to pray for me. As soon as she laid hands on me, I felt the presence of the Holy Spirit. His presence was so strong, I could not sit up straight in the chair. He directed my friend to lay her hands on my eyes and ask Him to show me what He wanted me to see.

Suddenly I was taken in the Spirit as the Lord revealed a heavenly vision. I saw a book. The Lord's hand reached out to open it, and several pages were turned. Then a bright light focused on the center of the page, highlighting certain words. As I peered curiously at the page, the writing slowly came into focus. I leaned in to read the words, and I saw my name written in gold. My name was recorded in the book! The Lord spoke to me: *Becca, your name is written in the Lamb's book of life. Your salvation is secure.* Feeling broken and at the same time filled with joy, I began to weep.

As I was lost in this place, Eddie Smith came and laid his hands on my eyes and said, "Lord, show her what You want her to see." Instantly another vision began to unfold. I saw an image of someone approaching on a cloud. As the image neared, I realized that it was Jesus. He was magnificent as the wind of the Holy Spirit encompassed Him and moved around Him. He was riding on the wind of the Spirit. His kingly robes and hair were flowing in the wind. It was as if time stood still. He looked at me and said, *Becca, your sins have been forgiven. Take up your cross, follow Me and sin no more. It is over. It is finished.*

I received the message that He was conveying to me. I accepted the fact that I am a child of the King saved through His grace. The torment of the enemy was over. From that moment on, I never again believed the lie or was tormented with the deception that my salvation was not secure. The depression and unworthiness ended at that moment.

Fear and unbelief are powerful strongholds, but the love of our Lord is an all-consuming love. When we seek Him with all our hearts and commit our ways to Him, the enemy must flee.

8. Walk in Integrity

The Hebrew word for *integrity* is *tom*. It means "blamelessness in regard to sin, a state or condition of moral purity." Scripture says that our integrity is our security: "The man of integrity walks securely, but he who takes crooked paths will be found out" (Proverbs 10:9); "Righteousness guards the man of integrity, but wickedness overthrows the sinner" (Proverbs 13:6).

When we walk uprightly, blameless before both man and God, we are safe under divine protection. As we go our way, we are well armed against the temptations of Satan, the troubles of the world and the accusations of man. Living a life of integrity and holiness sets the stage for us to walk in victory—and positions us to extend the Kingdom of God. It means that we have the character strength to face adversity, and even to rejoice in our trials, as Paul said:

Not only so, but we also rejoice in our sufferings, because we know that suffering produces perseverance; perseverance, character; and character, hope. And hope does not disappoint us, because God has poured out his love into our hearts by the Holy Spirit, whom he has given us.

Romans 5:3–5

Remember that this is a process. In order for character to be produced in us, there will be times when we have to lay down our own agendas. We might experience loss, hardship, broken relationships or various other troubles. The good news is that even in trials, tribulations and sufferings we can triumph. Actually we triumph not only *in* tribulation but *because* of tribulation. It is the trials of life that form character.

Not all development has to come through suffering, of course. The important thing to understand is that God is concerned with our growth. He is more concerned with our character than with our gifting. He will do what is needed for us to be in right relationship with Him.

Jesus said, "If anyone would come after me, he must deny himself and take up his cross daily and follow me. For whoever wants to save his life will lose it, but whoever loses his life for me will save it" (Luke 9:23–24).

As I shared regarding my experience, the Lord spoke clearly that I had to pick up my cross and follow Him. I had a part to play in walking out my salvation and allowing the Lord to form His character in me. This means dying daily to those things about us that do not line up with the Lord's standards. In this place of death, however, is life. In this place of intimacy is authority. In this place of surrender is freedom and liberty. In God's Kingdom, death produces strengthened, tested, proven character.

Enough Is Enough

We have looked at several steps that are necessary to take if we are going to walk in personal dominion. If you realize at this point that you are in need of freedom, begin to take the necessary action to achieve it. Press forward to work out your salvation with fear and trembling.

We will discuss in chapter 8 our roles as ambassadors for the King, but I want to note here that we carry royal authority that strikes fear in the ranks of darkness. God is challenging each of us to resound with the cry that "Enough is enough," and to take back all the enemy has stolen in our lives. We are called to be the examples to a lost world and extend the Kingdom of God. We cannot represent Kingdom dominion until we have established personal dominion.

6

MEASURE OF RULE

When we walk in a state of personal dominion, the Kingdom of God is made manifest.

This is usually evident in three different dimensions. First, wherever we are we represent the Kingdom. When we go to the grocery store or take a trip to a theme park, we represent Jesus. Because He lives in us by the power of the Holy Spirit, we are salt and light wherever we go.

Personal dominion means, next, that our specific habitats—our homes and places of work and neighborhoods—are part of the territory that we have a right to rule. Because we live and work in these areas, God gives us authority to make certain declarations about them.

And finally, the Lord also allots to each of us a special territory or assignment in which we have a physical presence and also spiritual authority. For some of us the territory might be an area—like the inner city or Wall Street. For others it might be a position: He places some strategically in leadership in schools, churches and governments. Still others find that their territories are people groups; some believers carry passion for runaways or drug addicts or the nations of the world. We may find that we have certain assignments only for specific seasons. We may also find that as we grow with God, He expands our realms of influence and spiritual authority.

Paul describes this stewardship in 2 Corinthians 10:13: "We will not boast of things without our measure, but according to the measure of the rule which God hath distributed to us, a measure to reach even unto you" (KJV).

The Greek word for *measure* is *metron*, which means "to cut out a space or distance with a measurer's reed or rule." It refers to the size or boundary of one's area of authority. The Greek word for *rule* is *kanon*, which refers to "a sphere of activity." Rule is the power one has within a particular, marked-out territory. The Greek word for *distribute* is *merizo*, which refers to "a division or share." Putting this all together we understand Paul to be saying that the Lord cordons off specific areas for each of His children in which we can move with power to make known the Kingdom of God. Paul's "measure of rule" was clear: His mission was to take the power of God to the territories of the Gentiles. This was Paul's assigned portion in which he was destined to rule.

The same process applies to you and me: We were created for dominion. It is exciting to know that the Lord has given each of us a portion on earth over which we have power to effect change. This should not be an entirely unfamiliar concept, however. At some point in our lives, we have all experienced this godly authority, a time when we discovered an innate ability to lead or a time when righteous indignation rose up in our spirits and brought about necessary changes. It might not be a daily occurrence, but there are times when unjust circumstances present themselves and something within us takes charge of the situation. This is part of the dominion DNA formed in us at creation.

Following Paul's Example

In discussing measure of rule, let's study Paul's visit to Athens on his second missionary journey, keeping in mind his call to the Gentiles. After ministering in Berea, Paul traveled to Athens in order to wait for Silas and Timothy to join him. During this time, he became distressed at the sight of idolatry and moral corruption. Taking advantage of this waiting period, he began to spread the message of the Gospel of Jesus Christ and the Kingdom of God.

Athens was a city famous for its religious and cultural diversity. Its hallmarks were intellectualism and paganism. Stoics and Epicureans represented the dominant belief systems of the region—although "gods" of other faith systems abounded. The Stoics held to pride and personal independence. Basically they were pantheistic: Nature was their god. The Epicureans sought pleasure. Their religious philosophy centered on experience, not reason. They were atheistic.

As Paul gave witness to the Gospel, many mocked the message and labeled him a babbler (see Acts 17:18). But above all, the Athenians loved to discuss new ideas and philosophies, so they took him to a meeting of the Areopagus, their official court, also known as Mars Hill. Intrigued, they asked him to expound upon his message. As he began to speak, he approached the door to their hearts and minds by stating the obvious: The Athenians were religious people. He noted further that they had erected an altar with this inscription: TO AN UNKNOWN GOD. Using divine wisdom he then cleverly sneaked through the open door by stating: "Now what you worship as something unknown I am going to proclaim to you" (verse 23). Paul became the messenger of the Unknown God and in doing so presented powerful truths of the Kingdom of God.

The Greek culture of Paul's day has many similarities with the cultures of our world today. Many of the beliefs and mindsets that challenge our Christian faith are the same ones that challenged Paul. Since our own measure of rule is always, ultimately, about the spread of the Kingdom, I want to note briefly the four points of his message. We can learn a great deal about sharing the Gospel from this example.

First, he stated that God is the Creator, disputing the Greeks' evolutionary theories concerning creation. Paul explained that from one man, Adam, all men were created. From this one man came all the nations of the earth. Second, he explained that God is sovereign: It was God who set the times and the places of these Athenians' lives so that they might find Him. To further his case, Paul quoted their own poets, showing how God is the answer to their deepest expression.

> "From one man he made every nation of men, that they should inhabit the whole earth; and he determined the times set for them and the exact places where they should live. God did this so that men would seek him and perhaps reach out for him and find him, though he is not far from each one of us. 'For in him we live and move and have our being.' As some of your own poets have said, 'We are his offspring.'"
>
> verses 26–28

Third, Paul revealed that his God is not a god of gold or silver; He is the Savior. He pointed out that their temples and idols were not divine in nature because they were man-made and, therefore, lacking in power. With all of their wisdom and searching, the Greeks had failed to find God.

Then, fourth, Paul stated that it was time for a decision. God has appointed a day of judgment. If they repented and turned to Jesus, they would experience salvation. If they rejected Jesus, they would be condemned eternally.

Paul knew his measure of rule and was faithful to his calling. Some rejected his message, but others were curious to hear more, and several were saved on the spot. As Paul presented the message of Jesus Christ, he gained a measure of authority. Because he used the *power* allotted to him in the *area* allotted to him, he was effective for the Kingdom.

The Magnitude of Our Calling

Paul's sermon on Mars Hill is a wonderful challenge to us—not only as an example of how to move in Kingdom dominion, but also as a plumb line for checking our own beliefs as we seek our proper roles. Do we really understand the dominion mandate given to our forefather Adam? Do we really believe that our God is a sovereign God? Do we accept the fact that He set the times and places of our lives?

We are not living in our neighborhoods and cities by mistake: God has put us there as Kingdom representatives. We are not supposed to wait for the Millennial reign of Christ to find our places; we are called to stand now for the Lord in the earth. Remember, measure of rule is tied to destiny, and destiny is linked to the dominion mandate of Adam.

It is time for us to shift out of the mindset that being a Christian is about going to church to feel good. Now it is

107

imperative that we be connected to a local church—a group of believers with whom there is accountability, covenant relationship and spiritual growth. We all need each other in the Body of Christ. But if we are going to achieve our deepest purposes, we have to go beyond this: The God-ordained plan for us individually and corporately is to be empowered in our relationships with the Lord and placed in our measure of rule, effecting change and establishing dominion.

Jesus gave us this calling in the Great Commission:

> Then Jesus came to them and said, "All authority in heaven and on earth has been given to me. Therefore go and make disciples of all nations, baptizing them in the name of the Father and of the Son and of the Holy Spirit, and teaching them to obey everything I have commanded you. And surely I am with you always, to the very end of the age."
>
> Matthew 28:18–20

We tend to read this as a directive to win lost souls—and stop there. We miss the bigger picture formed by these three strategic verses of Scripture.

Jesus spoke these words after obediently sacrificing Himself on the cross and conquering death. He was making the declaration that He is now the one with all authority in heaven and earth. Even though Satan has not yet received his eternal punishment, the judgment has been made: Satan has been found guilty and stripped of all authority. Satan has lost; Jesus has won.

It is time for us, the disciples of Christ, to make disciples of all nations. Remember that this commissioning was not a suggestion but a command from Jesus. He is positioned with all authority in heaven and on earth, and we—as a royal priesthood—are positioned with Him. There is not one believer who is excused or left out from this position. This is where our churches fall short. We have developed the mindset that it is the pastor's job to do all the work while the church members sit as spectators on the sidelines. When Jesus said, "I will give you the keys of the kingdom of heaven" (Matthew 16:19), He was speaking about all of His fellow heirs. We are ministers who are called to partner with Him in making disciples of all nations on the earth.

Making a disciple involves more than just making a convert. The Greek word for *disciple* is *matheteuo*. Being baptized and studying Scripture are primary factors in the discipling process, but it also involves a commitment of the will. In other words, a disciple "attaches" himself to the teacher—he lives with him, identifies with him and learns from him by both study and imitation.

The literal translation of *panta ethnos*—"all nations"— includes but is not limited to people. Thus when Jesus gave the directive for His followers to go to the nations and to disciple them, He was referring not just to the people but also to the land, government, leaders, rulers, businesses, families, schools and so on. The Church is to influence culture.

As Kingdom representatives, we should be establishing a righteous paradigm in our territories and areas of influence. We serve an awesome God. He is the Creator of the universe. He made us in His image as Kingdom ambassadors on this earth. We have available to us favor, creativity, power, wisdom, strategies and anything else we need to cause the lost world to be drawn to our God and cultures to be transformed. No matter where we are placed—in our homes, neighborhoods, businesses, churches—God has equipped and anointed us for the assignment.

Positioned for Rule

Now in order for us to legislate in our given territory, we have to demonstrate a presence. This means that our measure of rule has to know we are there. We cannot be hidden and gain authority. When dealing with people, for instance, we have to build trust before we will have access into their lives. Sometimes we have to show them Christ before we can talk about Christ.

When our three children were small, I wanted to help out with the family income, so I decided to give piano lessons in our home. It did not take long for the word to get out, and the afternoon slots began to fill quickly. Understanding that this was a territory the Lord was entrusting to me, I prayed that He would bring me the students who needed a revelation of the love of Jesus.

I received a phone call from a girl named Susie who was sixteen years old. She and her family were originally from Thailand. Her mother did not speak English but wanted to meet me before I became her daughter's music teacher. I agreed and scheduled an interview. The following afternoon as Susie and her mother entered our home, the Lord told me that I was to give her music lessons and also to believe for her salvation. He told me that this young girl had a powerful call on her life.

The interview was positive, and Susie soon began her music lessons. Before each scheduled lesson, I spent time in focused intercession for Susie's salvation. She was placed in my measure of rule, and it was my responsibility to see her brought into the Kingdom of God.

A couple of months passed, and my heart's cry grew stronger and more intense for her to come to salvation. Even so, I did not preach at her or force my beliefs on her. I simply treated her with love and built a relationship based on trust. One afternoon in the middle of a piece of music, Susie stopped suddenly and looked into my eyes.

"Miss Becca," she said, "can I ask you a question?"

"Yes, of course," I replied.

"You are a Christian, right?"

"Yes, I am. Why do you ask?"

"Your face glows with a presence," she said. "You are loving toward me, and I see Bible verses in your home. I also have Christian friends in my high school who have been talking to me about Jesus. I am curious to know Him, but my family worships Buddha. I know that he is a false god with no power. I do not want to change to another religion focused on the worship of a false god. I have to know that Jesus is real before I give my life to Him."

"Susie," I said, "Jesus is the one true Savior of the world. I know He wants to reveal Himself to you. Do you have a need in your life? We can pray and ask Jesus to help you. He will answer our prayer, and you will know that He is the one true God to be worshiped."

After a moment she said, "I do have a need. I lost my glasses two weeks ago. My parents were really mad at me because it was expensive to replace them. Then yesterday, I lost my new pair of glasses! I am afraid to tell my parents. Can we pray that I find my new pair before my parents discover that I lost them?"

"Absolutely," I responded. We then prayed in agreement asking the Lord to help Susie find her glasses.

Needless to say, I prayed that the Lord would miraculously reveal Himself to Susie and that her glasses would be found. The next week when Susie arrived for her lesson, she was beaming with excitement. Before I could ask what happened, she blurted her good news.

"Miss Becca, the day after we prayed, I went to school. After English class, my teacher called me to her desk and opened the desk drawer. She handed me a pair of glasses and asked if they were mine. Miss Becca, it was the first pair of glasses I had lost! Then that afternoon, the bus driver handed me a pair of lost glasses. They were the new pair of glasses my parents just bought for me! Not only did Jesus help me find my new pair of glasses, He also found my first pair of glasses. Can you lead me to Him? I know He is the one true God." We both wept tears of joy as Susie received Jesus as her Savior.

After Susie's salvation, she began to experience deep hunger for the Word of God. Greg and I got her a Bible and from that point forward, Susie and I spent the first portion of the music class working on piano lessons and the last portion studying Scripture. Her Buddhist parents would have forbidden her to read the Bible, so she stayed up late at night reading in bed under her sheets with a flashlight. Susie also began seeking the Lord for the purpose and calling on her life. He began to place an intercessory burden on her heart for her parents and all of her family members in Thailand who were trapped in the worship of Buddha. She yearned for them to come to salvation. God was moving powerfully in her life.

One day she told me that she was facing a difficult obstacle: Her parents were requiring her to go to the Buddhist temple to pray to Buddha and to receive a blessing from the Buddhist monk. She did not want to go, but was being made to do so. We prayed and asked the Lord to work mightily on her behalf.

The day came for her blessing from the monk. After her parents prayed to the idol of Buddha, the family was approached by a monk to pray a blessing over each of them.

Susie was the last family member to receive the blessing. He reached out to touch her shoulder, but his hand faltered. He looked into her eyes and attempted once more to put his hand on her shoulder, but it was as if something blocked her from his touch. He bowed to Susie, as if acknowledging the power within her, and left. God performed that miracle for Susie. In doing so, He also showed her the authority she carried in her measure of rule.

On the day of her last music lesson, Susie said, "Miss Becca, thank you for leading me to Jesus. I want you to know that when I graduate from college, I am going to Thailand as a missionary to lead my people to Him. I am to reach those gripped in darkness to the worship of Buddha." We both thanked the Lord for saving Susie, for His faithfulness in her life and for her calling to reach the Buddhist people of Thailand.

The Lord brought Susie to me, and while she was in my territory, I believed for her salvation. She met Jesus and was trained and equipped to understand her territory and measure of rule. She then went on to introduce others to Jesus and train them to discover their own measure of rule.

No matter what our assignment or measure of rule, if we recognize it and agree with the Lord about it, the discipling of nations will occur.

Resisting the Enemy—Forcefully

Not only do we work within our measure of rule to advance the Kingdom of God, but we also watch to see that the enemy does not enter and defile our territory or claim any hold over it. The Church must intercede and engage in strategic-level spiritual warfare prayer in order to defeat Satan's scheme on the earth. Actually, the Church's involvement in spiritual warfare prayer is part of the dominion mandate of Adam. Jesus has all authority over the earth, but we partner with Him by repenting for our sin and poor stewardship of the land, by rendering powerless the plans and schemes of the enemy, by cleansing the defiled land and by reestablishing dominion. The Lord is calling us not only to break the bondage from past defilement on the land, but to be on guard, resisting and refusing to accept further offensives of Satan and his army.

Jesus said, "From the days of John the Baptist until now, the kingdom of heaven has been forcefully advancing, and forceful men lay hold of it" (Matthew 11:12). John the Baptist came on the scene preaching aggressively for men to repent. He came in the spirit of Elijah, announcing the coming of the Messiah. He was preparing the way for the Kingdom of God just as we are called to manifest the Kingdom of God.

The traditional interpretation of this verse focuses on the nature of those who represent the Kingdom of God. Jesus indicates that His followers are forceful people who are committed to breaking away from sin and from the ways of the world to follow Jesus Christ. We walk in righteousness, earnestly seeking the Kingdom of heaven and all its power no matter the cost. One of the objectives of this stance is to resist the schemes of Satan that have corrupted the cultures of the world.

A less traditional interpretation of this verse is fascinating—and pertinent to our study. An Australian professor and expert in the Greek language, Dr. Ann Nyland has brought fresh insight to this verse as stated in *The Source New Testament*. The following is her translation: "From the time of John the Baptizer until now, Heaven's Realm is being used or even robbed by people who have no legal right to it. This stops those who do have legal right to it from enjoying their own property." This interpretation suggests that it is the enemy who is "forcefully advancing." The Greek word for this activity is *bia*. In her studies Dr. Nyland has discovered that this word refers to illegal, forcible acquisition or possession. Likewise, the Greek word for *lay hold* or *seize* is *harpazo*, which is defined as the illegal seizure of land.

This is the exact scheme of the enemy in the earth realm! As we have seen, he looks for those who will partner with him and, through man's cooperation, secures for himself what is ours. This confirms the need for the Church, the rightful, legal sons and daughters of God, to stand in the earth as co-heirs to this property, refusing any further possession of our domain.

Some years ago the Lord blessed our family with a brand-new home in a newly established neighborhood. It was a peaceful location with many Christian families; it was also a new field ripe for harvest. Several churches were planting congregations in the vicinity. It was a great place to live.

One day as we were driving through the neighborhood, Greg and I noticed a sign on the corner lot across from the elementary school. We both assumed it was announcing the building of a new church. Curious to find out, we went closer and read: "Future Home for the Mormon Church." This was not the spiritual influence that we desired to see established in our neighborhood.

Several days later as we passed the corner lot again, I told Greg that someone needed to do something about that Mormon church before they began to build on the land. With a smile he said, "You're right! So when are you going to deal with it?" His challenge surprised me. Even though I did not want a false religion established in our territory, I had not thought about dealing with it myself.

Greg was right. The Lord was calling us to stand on the land and refuse access to that false religion. The following Sunday as our family returned from church, we made a stop at the corner lot. Greg and I stood in front of the sign. I asked him if he wanted to pray. He replied, "No, you do it. I am here to agree with you as the Lord leads." What a privilege to be married to a man who blesses and releases the anointing in my life!

So I began to pray. It was not a lengthy prayer, as I knew what we were sent there to do.

"Father," I began, "we thank You for this beautiful neighborhood and all the families You have brought to live here. Father, we thank You for the work You are going to do in their lives. And right now we stand as legal landowners and homeowners in this territory. We stand as ones who have legal spiritual authority in this region. So right now in the name of Jesus we say that no Mormon church will be built in this neighborhood. We say no to the spirit of lying and error and all Antichrist and witchcraft spirits attached to the Mormon church. You do not have access, and you will not gain access into this territory. You are not welcome. We say no in Jesus' name. We speak to the finances that are funding the building of this church to dry up. We say that the required paperwork for this building will not go through and that the bank will not approve the loan. The door is shut to you right now. And, Father, we pray for all those who are involved in this Mormon church. We agree together that deception will be broken off of their minds and hearts, and that salvation will spring forth into their lives. We thank You ahead of time for their salvation. In Jesus' name we pray. Amen!"

Before leaving we poured anointing oil around the sign and claimed the land for the Kingdom of God. We made this declaration five years ago. To this day that Mormon church has not been built on the property; in fact, the sign has been removed. This is dominion—a cry arising from the followers of Jesus Christ that refuses illegal possession or seizure of land in our measure of rule. It is a declaration that resounds into the spirit realm: "Not in my city, not in my family, not in my territory, not on my watch!"

The world around us is waiting to be restored. There are lost souls who are searching for answers, land that needs to be cleansed and laws that need to be changed. In the next chapter we learn how to take our places in the Kingdom plan of God.

7

TAKING YOUR PLACE

It is exciting to discover that each of us plays a role in the reestablishment of God's original design for mankind and creation. As Jesus stated, "The time has come" (Mark 1:15). It is time for us to take our places as Kingdom ambassadors. You may be wondering where to begin or just what your area of influence is. We know that wherever we are, the Kingdom of God is also present. Even so, we have all been created for a purpose. It is time to become the Church that not only talks about how to effect change and transformation but is empowered to take action.

Get in There with God

There is a reason we exist. When God formed each of us, He had a plan in mind. We, like our Creator, have visions in our hearts. Many of us, however, live our lives without fully understanding our intended purpose.

Proverbs 29:18 is the familiar verse that tells us, in the King James Version, that without a vision the people perish. The NIV puts it this way: "Where there is no revelation, the people cast off restraint; but blessed is he who keeps the law." When there is no clear understanding of God's will and ways, then people lose their desire to walk within biblical standards. When we lose sight of Kingdom practices, then there is no vision to bring hope and direction. Our way is lost.

On the other hand, as we walk out our salvation and draw closer to God, He will impart the desire to follow His plan. As Paul said, "It is God who works in you to will and to act according to his good purpose" (Philippians 2:13). Not only does God give us the resolve and the determination to follow and please Him, but He also gives us the ability. The two work together. Our duty is divinely inspired. The following statement from *The Complete Biblical Library* is fast becoming one of my favorites: "The scriptural approach is not 'let go and let God,' but 'get in there with God.'" Friend, it is time to get in there with God and work for transformation in our territories.

The List of Excuses

Right now you might be tempted to rehearse in your mind what I term the list of excuses that disqualify you for the work of the Kingdom. Perhaps as you read these pages you are going down the checklist of all the reasons why the God-ordained plan for your life cannot be fulfilled. You might even be thinking that you are going to read these pages, but they will never apply to you. Doubts like these might surface: *I am not trained; I do not have a seminary or theological degree; I am not an outgoing, charismatic person; What do I possibly have to offer?* You might be picturing your family, your neighbors, your city and possibly the nations of the earth and thinking there is no possible way they can be redeemed and transformed. The job is too big.

Do you think you need great ability before you can begin? The saints and heroes of the past were not always people of great ability. Moses stuttered, and yet he took God's message to Pharaoh on behalf of the children of Israel. David was the youngest of his brothers and a shepherd, yet he defeated a giant and became a king, a man after God's own heart. Deborah was inspired by the Spirit with words that led Israel to wartime victory. Rahab was a prostitute who honored God's people and wound up as a player in Jesus' own genealogy. Jacob was changed. Paul was changed.

The same Holy Spirit who works in the great Christian leaders of today also works in each of us. Here is one of the most strategic statements you can grab hold of for dominion life: *Never allow your limitations to determine your future.* It is in our weaknesses that God makes us strong. In fact, if we think we can handle on our own what God is assigning to us, then we are in a dangerous place. We need Him in order to complete the task. Whatever God calls us to do will require total dependence on and faith in Him in order for it to be accomplished. God's dreams for us are even bigger than ours. He is entirely able to enlarge our personal capacities and capabilities. Instead of thoughts of inferiority and failure, a cry of trust and determination should resound in our hearts: *God, use me!*

121

To Him Who Is Faithful in Little

Jesus' parable of the talents shows us powerful scriptural truths concerning our abilities in God's Kingdom plan:

> "Again, it will be like a man going on a journey, who called his servants and entrusted his property to them. To one he gave five talents of money, to another two talents, and to another one talent, each according to his ability. Then he went on his journey."
>
> Matthew 25:14–15

The talent was the largest unit of currency in the ancient world. One denarius was almost equivalent to a workman's pay for one day, and one talent was equal to six thousand denarii. One talent was approximately twenty years of wages. Obviously there was a large amount of money at stake. This says a lot concerning the master's confidence in his servants and the tremendous amount of responsibility they had.

The Greek word used for *ability* is *dunamis*, which is also translated "power." This indicates that the servants had the power, authority and ability to accomplish a given task. The master was a wise man, discerning each man's level of authority and ability. The first servant was entrusted with one hundred years—a lifetime—of wages. The second servant was entrusted with forty years of wages, and the third servant with twenty years of wages. All three were entrusted with responsibility and given an opportunity for stewardship.

Just as the master in the story entrusted the stewardship of his property to the servants, so the Lord entrusts each of us with gifts, talents, money—all the things that go with a measure of rule.

Let's investigate how each servant handled his trusted amount:

"The man who had received the five talents went at once and put his money to work and gained five more. So also, the one with the two talents gained two more. But the man who had received the one talent went off, dug a hole in the ground and hid his master's money."

verses 16–18

The first two servants went out immediately, began to fulfill their assignment and doubled their money. Even though the third slave was put in charge of less, it did not mean he had less responsibility. But instead of fulfilling his assignment, he took the equally fearful and lazy steps of burying the talent in the ground.

Now after some time the master returned to settle accounts. I find it interesting that the master did not return at once. He was giving the servants plenty of time to increase the talents. The same is true for each of us. The Lord delays His return, giving us the opportunity to do His Kingdom business.

When the day came to give account of their stewardship, the first two servants showed that they were devoted to their master: They had doubled the money entrusted to them. These two received their master's praise and were put in charge of many things. The realm they were given to rule far surpassed the original amount with which they were entrusted. They would now have room for increased responsibility and greater opportunities to use their gifts, abilities, influence and money.

The third servant, however, did not receive the blessing of the master.

"Then the man who had received the one talent came. 'Master,' he said, 'I knew that you are a hard man, harvesting where you have not sown and gathering where you have not scattered seed. So I was afraid and went out and hid your talent in the ground. See, here is what belongs to you.'

"His master replied, 'You wicked, lazy servant! So you knew that I harvest where I have not sown and gather where I have not scattered seed? Well then, you should have put my money on deposit with the bankers, so that when I returned I would have received it back with interest. Take the talent from him and give it to the one who has the ten talents."

verses 24–28

Here we have an example of one who allowed his list of excuses, disqualifiers and limitations to undermine his future inheritance. When he approached his master, he was defensive and tried to shift the blame. He accused his master of suspect business practices instead of owning up to his weakness and laziness. As a result he lost his responsibility, position and opportunity to grow in his master's domain.

The one who is faithful with a few things will be put in charge of many things. What a powerful example of the Kingdom! Those who use their gifts, abilities, talents, money, and the like in obedience to the Lord in their measure of rule will be blessed and positioned to receive more—more of Him, more of His presence, more of His goodness, more of His righteousness, more of His authority and more of His territory.

You see, God is always about His business. As we are faithful in the fields assigned to us and as we grow in depth and maturity, the Lord will enlarge the boundaries of our tents. God is always taking us deeper and higher in Him. The more we grow in relationship with Him and with those around us, the more territory and lives we affect.

This is our mission—to take our places in the Kingdom and enter into the powerful work of ruling with the Lord in our fields of responsibility. Here are four points to get us started.

1. Seek First the Kingdom of God

The highest priority is to be in intimate communion with God. Everything in our walk with the Lord stems from this personal relationship. It is in this place that we hear God's voice and discern the God-ordained assignments for our lives. As Jesus instructed, "Seek first his kingdom and his righteousness, and all these things will be given to you as well" (Matthew 6:33).

Leading up to this verse, Jesus was teaching on the topic of money and the worry revolving around physical and spiritual needs being met. We are to seek His Kingdom and righteousness, and He will take care of our needs.

The word *seek* suggests being continually absorbed in a search for something, or making a strenuous and diligent effort to obtain something. This is the intensity with which we should try to obtain the demonstrated rule and power of God in our lives. Through the Holy Spirit we seek to obey the commands of Jesus, to possess His righteousness, to remain separate from the world and to show Christ's love to everyone. When this is our greatest desire, we will naturally wish to be obedient to His purposes. It will then follow that we will be empowered to receive His strategies and to fulfill them. It is through our personal relationship with the Lord—seeking His Kingdom—that every spiritual blessing comes.

2. Pray for His Kingdom to Come

When we are in right relationship with God, the next most crucial ingredient for taking our places in the Kingdom of God is a faithful prayer life. Prayer is behind all great moves of God. It is through prayer that we influence history. Here are a few quotes by great spiritual leaders in recent history concerning the value of prayer:

"Beware in your prayers, above everything else, of limiting God, not only by unbelief, but by fancying that you know what He can do. Expect unexpected things 'above all that we ask or think.'"

Andrew Murray

"God does nothing but by prayer, and everything with it."

John Wesley

"Prayer does not fit us for the greater work; prayer is the greater work."

Oswald Chambers

"Every great movement of God can be traced to a kneeling figure."

D. L. Moody

"If the church would only awaken to her responsibility of intercession, we could well evangelize the world in a short time. It is not God's plan that the world be merely evangelized ultimately. It should be evangelized in every generation. There should be a constant gospel witness in every corner of the world so that no sinner need close his eyes in death without hearing the gospel, the good news of salvation through Christ."

T. S. Hegre

And Jesus gave us these transforming words:

"Pray, then, in this way: 'Our Father who is in heaven, hallowed be Your name. Your kingdom come. Your will be done, on earth as it is in heaven. Give us this day our daily bread.

And forgive us our debts, as we also have forgiven our debtors. And do not lead us into temptation, but deliver us from evil. [For Yours is the kingdom and the power and the glory forever. Amen.]'"

Matthew 6:9–13, NASB

Jesus taught us to pray that the Kingdom of God will come, and that the King's agendas and standards will be established on earth just as they are in heaven. As we have noted, this is not reserved for the Millennium. It expresses a desire for God to rule in every heart now so that God's will may always be done on earth as it is in heaven.

Praying for the spiritual presence and manifestation of the Kingdom of God now includes walking in God's authority against the works and schemes of Satan, praying for the sick, reaching the lost, promoting righteousness, walking in the love of the Lord, standing in our regions and territories and playing a role in transformation. We are to seek the Lord diligently and to pray that His Kingdom will be made known on the earth today.

Friend, I desire more of God now. What an awesome day it could be to live in a measure of rule where our prayers pave the way for transformation and revival! Through our prayers and faithfulness to God, this can be a reality.

3. Commit Your House to the Lord

We discussed in chapter 5 the dynamics of a home life that lead to personal dominion. Here we focus on serving and worshiping the Lord and serving and honoring each other in our homes. The truth is, the Christian home is not very different from a non-Christian home. Divorce, adultery, abuse and other forms of ungodliness have invaded our families.

But the Bible teaches us that we all have the responsibility of Kingdom stewardship over our homes and families.

Like Joshua we have to determine to follow the path of righteousness: "But as for me and my household," he said, "we will serve the LORD" (Joshua 24:15). Each believer must continually choose whom he or she will follow and serve. Time after time, we have to make the choice to persevere in faith and to obey the Lord. As we walk in fear of the Lord and His ways, placing Him first in our lives, submitting to Him and to one another in love and raising our children in the ways of the Lord, we are stewarding His Kingdom within the family life.

A husband-and-wife relationship takes work. We must pray together, grow together spiritually and emotionally and simply spend time together. We must serve, love and submit one to another in honor and respect. Even in the midst of our busy schedules, we have to set time aside to focus on this relationship. Now we all know marriage is a give-and-take relationship, but when both spouses come into marriage with the attitude of loving and serving the other, then joy, happiness and peace will reign.

As parents we have to establish Kingdom standards with our children. We must love, encourage, protect, teach, pray for and discipline them. It is our responsibility to take them to church, share the Gospel message of Jesus Christ and provide a home in which the Lord is exalted. As we pour into our children the love of the Lord, we are preparing them for their God-ordained purpose on earth.

The following story written by Jill Carattini points out the importance of faith in the home.

At a funeral service in 1742, two giants of the faith stood beside their mother's graveside. John Wesley conducted the services; his brother Charles Wesley wrote the epitaph for the tombstone.

Susanna Wesley was a woman her husband called "the best of mothers." Writing to his children, he described his wife as one they had to thank above all for "the wholesome and sweet motherly advice and counsel which she has often given you to fear God."

Determined that her children would know and love Christ, Susanna made sure that such guidance was a regular part of her children's lives. With each child she reserved a specific day and time each week to sit and discuss matters of God and things on their hearts. The time spent together was cherished by all, such that many continued the discussions with their mother into adulthood through letter-writing. Once asking his mother for a definition of sin, John Wesley received a response fit for theology books. "Take this rule," she wrote to John. "Whatever weakens your reason, impairs the tenderness of your conscience, obscures your sense of God, or takes off your relish of spiritual things; in short, whatever increases the strength and authority of your body over your mind, that thing is sin to you, however innocent it may be in itself."

Susanna was incredibly bright and taught her children the joy of disciplined learning. Having an opportunity for education available to few women of her time, as a young woman Susanna seized the occasion. While her husband was away preaching, Susanna adopted the practice of reading sermons from the library aloud to her family. Word of the weekly meetings held in her kitchen quickly spread, until over two hundred were gathering regularly, and the parsonage could hardly contain those who came to hear. It was in such a setting that John, who would become the fervent preacher, and Charles, who would become the great hymnist, were raised.

129

Though her life was marked by a determined pursuit of God, it was also marked with hardship. Nine of the nineteen children born to Samuel and Susanna Wesley died in infancy. Two different times their home was destroyed by fire, one time nearly taking John's life. And they lived in severe poverty. Yet her determined faith was one she insisted on sharing, and perhaps for this · reason there was not a greater force upon eighteenth-century England than her children.

> "With God, the Impossible Is Possible," by Ravi Zacharias, A Slice of Infinity, No. 42, originally printed 29 February 2000 (www.rzim.org). Used by permission of Ravi Zacharias International Ministries.

4. Take Action in Your "World"

Within our various walks are different assignments and spheres of authority assigned to different people—and these can change in different seasons. Some are called to move with Kingdom power in their neighborhoods. Some have impact on the workplace. Some have authority within the government. Others affect lives and regions through churches and ministries. Still others work for spiritual and social transformation in their cities or states or nations.

The final point is obedience to the Lord and what He is calling us to do within the territory He has given us to rule. As Paul said, "Now it is required that those who have been given a trust must prove faithful" (1 Corinthians 4:2). As stewards of the Kingdom in our measure of rule, we are expected to work faithfully and diligently.

The following stories show how the Lord used ordinary people like you and me to have an impact in their measure of rule. It is my prayer that these encounters will inspire you to begin to take action in your area of influence.

Influence in a College Dorm

As a college student, Joseph Winger found that his "territory" happened to be the fourth floor of his small dormitory. He and two other Christians began meeting at midnight every Monday through Thursday for prayer and Scripture reading.

By the end of the next semester, more than twenty students were gathering at midnight four nights each week to encounter God. He showed up, and everyone on the floor was touched by an outpouring of the Holy Spirit. Backsliders returned to the Lord. Nominal Christians were ignited with a love for Him. Some students met Jesus for the first time. Believers and unbelievers alike were all aware that the Lord's presence invaded that long, narrow hall. What began with three young believers uniting in consistent prayer turned into a life-changing revival.

Influence in Branson, Missouri

In Branson, Missouri, a group of pastors from different denominations began meeting together for prayer early in 1996. Initially part of a pastors' prayer summit in conjunction with International Renewal Ministries, they continued to meet one Wednesday every month. They began to develop relationships of love, trust and common purpose.

A few years passed. One morning as the pastors gathered, they received the news that the tragic Columbine High School shooting had just taken place. They agreed that they should go immediately to their own high school to pray. One of the pastors contacted the principal to explain that the group was coming to pray in the parking lot. The principal's response was to invite the clergy to come inside the high school and pray. "We need your prayers," he said. Upon arriving they were welcomed and taken to the conference room.

From that day on the pastors have been meeting in the conference room of the high school the first Wednesday of every month. Many times school administrators join them. This has given the pastors access into other schools in Branson as well—and favor. Youth pastors, for example, are welcomed onto school campuses to meet with students and have lunch together.

At one point the school district's superintendent stepped down. When the job placement agency explained that it would begin by talking with different focus groups in the community to see what qualities were desirable in a replacement, the school board asked them to meet first with that group of praying pastors. As a result, the ministers' input was instrumental in the search for a new superintendent.

A strong Christian was hired. He told the student body that he expected them to bring their Bibles to school and read them. He set a righteous standard.

In addition, a Christian businessman has been invited into the city to provide training for all businesses in the area of management and management-labor relationships. The training is titled Servant Leadership and is based on Christian principles with the Bible as the guide. More than fifty of the Fortune 500 companies use his guidance. In Branson, at last count, 23 businesses had embraced this Servant Leadership model, including the school system and local hospital. Each month, a character trait from Scripture such as love, honesty, peace or integrity becomes the focus for all of these businesses. Employees and students citywide are taught the importance of functioning in this character trait. In essence the Bible is being taught in these 23 businesses. The city is laying a foundation for following Christ.

Influence in Boise, Idaho

Scripture says that where brethren dwell together in unity, the Lord commands a blessing (see Psalm 133). This is exactly what pastors, prayer leaders, businessmen and women and governmental leaders have found in the city of Boise, Idaho, also known as Treasure Valley.

In 1991 a group of pastors from the Treasure Valley gathered in the mountains north of Boise for a Pastors' Prayer Summit. They asked the Lord to help them come into unity so they could reach out cooperatively in their city with the Gospel message. From that time, the pastors have continued to meet weekly and plan annual prayer summits. They have also joined with other prayer leaders, forming a network of 280 prayer warriors who intercede for the city on a consistent basis.

In the meantime, a Treasure Valley Festival with Luis Palau was planned. This festival involved a large group of businessmen and women, pastors and representatives from many different churches. Prayer rallies, prayer walks, counselor training sessions, a rally for the youth and other events all helped prepare for the weekend event.

More than 370 Treasure Valley churches participated in the festival, the largest Christian event held in Idaho. More than 100,000 people attended. Some 4,500 booklets describing how to receive Christ were given out; 1,200 people made decisions for Christ. Hundreds of volunteers from many different churches worked side by side counseling, setting up and taking down equipment, praying and helping in the children's and youth areas.

Cooperative efforts like these have encouraged those who pray for Boise, have brought increased unity among the churches, have brought favor to and built relationships between government leaders and the church and have added several thousand new converts to area churches.

United in Arkansas City, Kansas

This section would not be complete without taking the opportunity to acknowledge how the Lord is working in Arkansas City, Kansas—the heartland of America. I have had the privilege of ministering and teaching there and participating in the prayer focus of this state. The following is just one of many miraculous events that began unfolding in the past couple of years for Sandy Newman and Deeann Ward of Destiny Ministries and Gateway Prayer House.

In February 2005 Sandy and Deeann attended a Christian conference in which Chuck Pierce spoke this word: "This is the year for Kansas: The whirlwinds will blow and root up the root of abortion and innocent bloodshed. Get a strategy." Both Sandy and Deeann believed the word of the Lord and began to seek Him and His agendas for their state.

The extensive spiritual mapping and research that followed this prophetic word regarding bloodshed in the state proved to be valuable in releasing Kansas's birthright—a birthright being God's designed inheritance for a person or place. The mapping included studying God's design, weaving natural and spiritual laws together and applying them to problems in every arena of society. The spiritual mapping team discovered that Kansas is home to one of the largest abortion clinics in the United States. Actually, Wichita, Kansas, is known as the abortion capital of the United States.

The team also focused on the state's role in displacing Native Americans. Arkansas City was one of the nine cities in the United States that served as a starting point and checkpoint for the land run into Oklahoma. More than forty thousand people came to Kansas to rush into Oklahoma, taking the land the Cherokee people called home. This First Nation tribe was removed from its land and forced into reservations. There were also Indian massacres that occurred throughout the state.

As these historical facts were uncovered, Sandy, Deeann and their intercessors began to pray on the land where these defilements occurred. They repented for these atrocities and asked God to cleanse and redeem the land.

The Lord began to move supernaturally and answer the prayers of this group of believers. He connected them with Christian Native American leaders in the United States, including Jay Swallow. Amazing things happened along the way that culminated in a historic Native American reconciliation.

A meeting was scheduled to seek the Lord further concerning the state. As the meeting dates approached, the Lord spoke to Sandy to make an unusual purchase: He told her to buy a buffalo as a gift to Jay, as the buffalo hunters from Kansas had killed off most of the Native American buffalo. Three days before the event, the Lord connected Sandy with a buffalo rancher. She bought a buffalo for Jay as a gesture from the heart to continue to restore the Native Americans' stolen inheritance in Kansas and throughout the United States.

As the buffalo was presented to Jay, he began to weep. Chuck Pierce was also in this meeting and said that it was probably one of the most healing acts our nation had ever done. He went on to prophesy that they had witnessed a layer of America's shield of faith restored, and that this would prevent the next terrorist attack destined to come to this land. Three

weeks later we heard the report of liquid bombs being uncovered in airplanes that were headed for American cities.

During this time, Deeann prophesied to one of the church members that he was to run for city commissioner of Arkansas City. He went the next day and put his name on the ballot. He received such a high percentage of the vote during the election that he was invited to serve as mayor and is now leading the city in a governmental and spiritual position.

As a result of these and many other events, there are now more than one hundred church leaders, intercessors and ministers throughout Kansas who meet together with Sandy and Deeann quarterly for the purpose of praying and seeking the Lord and making plans for their state. Leaders are standing together, strategizing and believing for revival and transformation.

God can, does and will do amazing things when we hear His voice, see what He is doing and begin to execute His plans in the territories He has allotted us.

What If?

I have a question for us to consider: What if? What if we all took our places in our measures of rule? What if we all began to function in our rightful positions in our homes, neighborhoods, schools, workplaces, ministries, churches, cities, states or nations? What if we all began to embrace the truth of "getting in there with God" and not allowing our limitations to determine our future? What if we chose as believers to walk in unity with the common goal of transformation and revival? What if we began to walk in dominion and backed the enemy into a corner?

Let's be believers who faithfully steward our measure of rule and multiply and occupy our territory.

8

AUTHORITY OF BELIEVERS

Because we are heirs of the Kingdom of God, we have the legal right as His representatives to exert power over the enemy in the name of Jesus. And we have territorial rights, too. Put generally, legal power usually involves a certain jurisdiction, and jurisdiction implies the ability to administer justice in a particular area.

The apostle Paul explains the basis for our position: "We are therefore Christ's ambassadors, as though God were making his appeal through us" (2 Corinthians 5:20). We are ambassadors—the personal representation—of the heavenly Kingdom to the earthly kingdom. This means that we have Christ's authority throughout the whole realm of earth! God works directly through us to combat the works of evil and darkness and to spread the glorious message of the Gospel of Christ.

Two Revelations to Peter

For our study of our authority in Christ, let's start with the exchange between Jesus and Peter on the subject of who Jesus is:

> Now when Jesus went into the region of Caesarea Philippi, He asked His disciples, Who do people say that the Son of Man is? And they answered, Some say John the Baptist; others say Elijah; and others Jeremiah or one of the prophets. He said to them, But who do you [yourselves] say that I am? Simon Peter replied, You are the Christ, the Son of the living God. Then Jesus answered him, Blessed (happy, fortunate, and to be envied) are you, Simon Bar-Jonah. For flesh and blood [men] have not revealed this to you, but My Father Who is in heaven. And I tell you, you are Peter [Greek, Petros—a large piece of rock], and on this rock [Greek, petra—a huge rock like Gibraltar] I will build My church, and the gates of Hades (the powers of the infernal region) shall not overpower it [or be strong to its detriment or hold out against it]. I will give you the keys of the kingdom of heaven; and whatever you bind (declare to be improper and unlawful) on earth must be what is already bound in heaven; and whatever you loose (declare lawful) on earth must be what is already loosed in heaven.
>
> Matthew 16:13–19, AMP

Here we have the core confession of the Body of Christ: It is Simon Peter's proclamation that Jesus is the Christ, the Son of the living God. Jesus commended Peter because this was a spiritual revelation that could have come only from our Father in heaven.

Jesus then made an amazing proclamation of His own to Simon Peter: "And I tell you that you are Peter, and on this rock I will build my church" (verse 18). I like the Amplified Bible translation of this verse, because it explains so clearly what Jesus was conveying. Simon Peter, the first to make this Kingdom confession, was the first to receive the promise that God would use him like a large piece of rock upon which to build.

Then it gets even better. Jesus stated that joining Peter would be other believers who would also proclaim this truth and represent the Kingdom of God. Together this Body would make up a huge rock—*petra*—like Gibraltar, and on this great rock He would build His Church. What is this rock? It is the revelation, confession and proclamation that Jesus is the Christ, the Son of the living God. Remember that we discussed in chapter 4 how the rocks split when Jesus gave up His Spirit on the cross. He is the new King, the new government, the new foundation. He is the Rock of our salvation.

Now in the next few statements made by Jesus, we see that immediately following His proclamation about the Church, He focused on the position of authority in which the Church is to operate. Let's look again at His words:

"The gates of Hades (the powers of the infernal region) shall not overpower it [or be strong to its detriment or hold out against it]. I will give you the keys of the kingdom of heaven; and whatever you bind (declare to be improper and unlawful) on earth must be what is already bound in heaven; and whatever you loose (declare lawful) on earth must be what is already loosed in heaven."

verses 18–19 AMP

As I read these verses, a sense of awe and fervent excitement rises within my Spirit. Here we have revealed to us our

139

authority as ambassadors, kings and priests. Let's investigate several different meanings of these keys and their significance. I am indebted to the *Theological Dictionary of the New Testament* (Eerdmans, 1964–1976) for fleshing out a number of researched materials I have used in this next section.

Keepers of the Keys

The first key of authority that relates to our study is the key to heaven. In the ancient world, and also in parts of our modern world, it was believed that heaven is closed off by doors, and that certain deities or angelic beings possess the keys. In Babylonian depictions, for example, Shamash held the key to heaven in his left hand. In Italy, Janus held the key. In Mithraism, a mystery religion that was active in Roman culture, Kronos held the key. In later Judaism, Michael the angelic prince is called the keeper of the keys.

Jesus alluded to heaven's key when He stated, "In truth I tell you, there were many widows in Israel in the days of Elijah, when *the heavens were closed up* for three years and six months, so that there came a great famine over all the land" (Luke 4:25, AMP, emphasis added). The general belief was that the heavens were closed because the door to rain was shut and locked with a key held by God. He chooses when to bless with rain and when to withhold rain. An interesting verse in Revelation shows us that God will one day entrust these keys to His messengers: The two witnesses of the last days "have power to shut up the sky so that it will not rain during the time they are prophesying" (Revelation 11:6).

Another common view regarding keys of authority is that the underworld, Hades, is barred by gates. Whoever holds the keys has power over the underworld. For the Babylonians, Nedu was the keeper of the underworld and guarded the locks. Kronos held the key in Mithraism. In magic literature Anubis plays this role. Jewish tradition taught that the keys to forty thousand gates of the last hell are in God's hands.

We know, of course, that Jesus overcame death and Hades: "Do not be afraid. I am the First and the Last. I am the Living One; I was dead, and behold I am alive for ever and ever! And I hold the keys of death and Hades" (Revelation 1:17–18). Death and Hades lost possession of the keys. Jesus now holds the keys and, with them, the power and authority over death and Hades.

In Revelation 3:7 we learn that Jesus, as the offshoot of David, holds the key of the Davidic line: "These are the words of him who is holy and true, who holds the key of David. What he opens no one can shut, and what he shuts no one can open." As the King of all kings, Christ holds the key to the eternal Kingdom and the eternal life that exists there. His sovereignty is unlimited; His rule extends over *all* powers, authorities and dominions.

Jesus referred to another key of authority—the key of knowledge—when He confronted the Pharisees concerning their false witness: "Woe to you experts in the law, because you have taken away the key to knowledge. You yourselves have not entered, and you have hindered those who were entering" (Luke 11:52). This key unlocks the door to the knowledge or understanding that leads to salvation and revelation of the Kingdom of God. There is power in the truth of the Word of God. When this truth is kept hidden and the door of knowledge kept shut, souls are prevented from salvation. But when the truth of the Gospel message is proclaimed, many walk through the opened door of salvation into the Kingdom of God.

This leads us to the keys of the Kingdom that were promised to Peter and to all of us in the Church. We see that keys of authority are used to unlock a door or gate and, therefore, represent the power to keep in or to let out. These keys control the locks in the doors of death, Hades and the evil schemes of darkness, as well as the doors of heaven, the knowledge of God and the key of David, meaning complete royal and sovereign reign over all God's Kingdom. *Kingdom*, remember, refers to royal power, dominion or rule. It involves the right or authority to rule. Jesus placed the keys of the Kingdom in the hands of the Church.

In other words, we have access to and the right to use the keys now.

The Authority to Bind and Loose

What are the specific keys with which we have been entrusted?

We noted previously that Jesus corrected the Pharisees for not fulfilling their task of leading, opening the door or making a way into the Kingdom of God through their teaching of the Scriptures. They kept the door shut. The Lord, therefore, turned the keys over to Peter and all believers. In the Bible and in Jewish teaching, handing over keys implies the appointment to full authority. But what is our particular appointment? Jesus said that He would give us the authority to bind and loose.

This idea of binding and loosing was used commonly by rabbis. They spoke of binding and loosing as forbidding or permitting. It is judicial authority. We have, therefore, the authority as Jesus' representatives to administer justice in cases held in the heavenly court of law. This is done in partnership with the Lord and in obedience to Him.

As Christians we do not have the legal right to tell God what to do, but we do have the legal right, authority and power to forbid what the Lord directs us to forbid and to release and welcome what He has designed for us to set free. In other words, we have the right to forbid on earth what is already found guilty and forbidden in heaven, and we have the right to permit on earth what is found right and permitted in heaven. You see, when you and I rise out of bed in the morning, the enemy and powers of darkness should come to attention and take notice. They should be on guard, thinking, *Oh, no! What are they going to do to bring us harm today?*

The exciting news is we have the daily direction of the Lord through the power of the Holy Spirit who speaks to us and enlightens the written Word of God. Friend, the Lord has already pronounced the final judgment against Satan and his ranks of darkness. They have not yet experienced the day when they will receive the sentence of imprisonment and be thrown into the abyss for eternity, but they have already been defeated at the cross. They no longer hold keys of authority. Through Jesus the Kingdom of God has been restored in our personal lives and in creation.

As we receive direction from Jesus, the keeper of the keys, we have the judicial authority as His Kingdom ambassadors to stand in the earth for Him and to execute His plans. We will discuss this further in the next chapter, but this statement is so important for us to grasp I want to repeat it here as well: The key to our effectiveness is to walk in humility before the Lord and be obedient to do what we see the Father doing. When our Kingdom plans are His plans for that time, then we have the authority to effect change. If, on the other hand, we plan our own agendas and ask God to bless them, there will be no lasting fruit. It is not our job to direct Jesus; we look to Him to give us the blueprints sketched in His throne room. As we submit to, follow and build His

Kingdom plan, we will be effective. Change, transformation and revival will come.

Watchmen on the Walls

We understand, then, that we have the authority to bind and loose on earth what we see patterned for us in heaven. The Lord wants us to take back all that we have handed over to the enemy and all that he has stolen. How do we go about this task? We act as the watchmen and gatekeepers in the land.

In biblical days a watchman was one who stood on the walls of Jerusalem or in the watchtowers to observe whatever was coming toward the city. The Hebrew word for *watchman* is *sopeh*. It is translated "lookout, guard, sentinel, sentry, armor, protection, security, shield, keeper or turnkey of one's territory." Anything that this person saw approaching, either good or bad, would be announced. Naturally it was vital that he warn of coming danger. He had to remain on the alert for any hostile advances against the city—particularly at night. The night watches were the most likely times of attack.

We are also watchmen in our territories. We must be on alert and see what is approaching in our personal lives and our territories before it arrives at the gate of entrance. Standing on the wall for us is a spiritual stance; it is the Holy Spirit who reveals the spiritual activity around us.

I was recently leading a prayer meeting. As we were praying, the Lord revealed to me a vision of the Church. I saw an army standing in rows of perfectly formed lines. The soldiers were clothed in armor and standing at ease. They were just standing there. They were in line formation, but they were not moving or on the alert. It was as if the soldiers in the army were in formation because they knew they were supposed to be there, but they were passive in their stance and not fulfilling their duty.

Suddenly I heard a heavenly command: *Attention!* As the command was released, every soldier in that formation came sharply to attention. The command awoke and aroused the army. It seemed to awaken their spirits to become alert and ready for their orders and assignments. I heard the Lord say, *It is time to be alert, to awaken from your position of just standing in place and come to attention before the King. It is time to stand in authority, to hear and receive your assignments and to advance.*

As the Lord was speaking this vision, one of the men praying with us began to read these words from the book of Ezekiel:

The word of the LORD came to me: "Son of man, speak to your countrymen and say to them: 'When I bring the sword against a land, and the people of the land choose one of their men and make him their watchman, and he sees the sword coming against the land and blows the trumpet to warn the people, then if anyone hears the trumpet but does not take warning and the sword comes and takes his life, his blood will be on his own head. Since he heard the sound of the trumpet but did not take warning, his blood will be on his own head. If he had taken warning, he would have saved himself. But if the watchman sees the sword coming and does not blow the trumpet to warn the people and the sword comes and takes the life of one of them, that man will be taken away because of his sin, but I will hold the watchman accountable for his blood.'

"Son of man, I have made you a watchman for the house of Israel; so hear the word I speak and give them warning from me. When I say to the wicked, 'O wicked man, you will surely die,' and you do not speak out to dissuade him from his ways, that wicked man will die for his sin, and I will hold you accountable for his blood. But if you do warn the wicked man to turn from his ways and he does not do so, he will die for his sin, but you will have saved yourself.

"Son of man, say to the house of Israel, 'This is what you are saying: "Our offenses and sins weigh us down, and we are wasting away because of them. How then can we live?"' Say to them, 'As surely as I live, declares the Sovereign LORD, I take no pleasure in the death of the wicked, but rather that they turn from their ways and live. Turn! Turn from your evil ways! Why will you die, O house of Israel?'"

Ezekiel 33:1–11

The Lord has given to each of us a responsibility to watch, a directive to stand on the wall to see what is approaching, to announce it and to blow the trumpet. As we stand in a place of prayer, watching on the wall and hearing the voice of the Lord, we can announce and release His directions and commands. We can reveal the presence of the enemy and welcome the presence of the Lord. When we are rightly positioned in our territory or sphere of influence, we can establish a place of habitation of the Lord and reach the lost with the Good News of the Gospel.

Gatekeepers for the City

As the watchman stands on the wall and sees who is approaching, he reports to the gatekeeper: "Then the watchman saw another man running, and he called down to the gatekeeper, 'Look, another man running alone!'" (2 Samuel 18:26). The gatekeeper is the one who tends and guards the gate. He has the authority to control access through the city walls. If he does not open the gate, then entrance to the city is not allowed. If he opens the gate, entrance is permitted. In Bible days, gatekeepers were Levites, Temple

146

officers. They were guardians both of the city and of private houses.

In one of Jesus' parables, He described the porter, or gate-keeper, as someone who was also responsible to watch: "The Son of Man is as a man taking a far journey, who left his house, and gave authority to his servants, and to every man his work, and commanded the porter to watch" (Mark 13:34, KJV). The following is an example of the watchman and the gatekeeper working together in a city.

Authority in Action

We were living in the city of Houston. I was involved with a unified group of intercessors in the city who were standing in prayer and intercession concerning the high crime rate. As we prayed we noted that the city began reporting a decline in crime. The rate was so dramatic, in fact, the police department was interviewed by the media. Representatives from police departments in various other cities came to learn the success-ful plans and strategies from the Houston department in order to implement them in their own cities. The funny thing was, the Houston police department could not give a reason for the decreased crime rate; they had not implemented any new crime prevention plans. They were grateful for the decrease, but had no explanation as to why it had occurred.

Now those of us praying knew the answer! We were pray-ing in authority in our measure of rule, standing against law-lessness and death and loosing righteousness and obedience. Our prayers were being heard in heaven, and the enemy's hand was being weakened. We were elated and filled with faith.

Then one evening it was announced on the news that a serial killer was loose and roaming the streets of Houston. He had already killed three women, and the police were looking for any leads. Within a week, another report was broadcast that the killer had struck again, violently murdering his fourth victim. Fear, death and lawlessness were gaining a grip in the city.

Within a couple of days, the police spoke on the evening news asking again for any leads from the community. They were concerned that this man was preparing to kill again, and they had no clues to his whereabouts. They were urging the citizens of the city to be cautious and not be out alone late at night. We were instructed to keep doors and windows locked. This report was released the same evening of our regular prayer meeting. As ones who had been standing against violence in the city, we were not going to lie down and allow fear, death and lawlessness access without a fight.

As we prayed that evening, we asked the Lord to send His warring angels to battle over the city against the forces of darkness. We stood firm in the belief that the man would be caught. We decreed that murdering and lawlessness would end that evening. We declared that the necessary leads to catch this man would be given to the police. We commanded fear, death, violence and murder to leave the city in Jesus' name, and we shut the demonic spiritual gate over the city, forbidding access to those spirits. This was our territory, so we became watchmen and gatekeepers. We took our rightful positions as Kingdom ambassadors with the keys of the Kingdom in our hands and legislated Kingdom authority in our realm.

We arrived home in time to watch the ten o'clock news. As the news began the first words out of the commentator's mouth were a statement that the serial killer had been arrested that evening. The police had received a phone call from a woman reporting the strange behavior of a man in her neighborhood. The police responded quickly and caught the man, who was minutes from taking a fifth victim.

I began to shout with joy, and our phone began to ring as other church members heard the same report. Just at the time we were warring in intercession against murder, fear and death and proclaiming that this man would be caught, he was. The events were unfolding within the same hour that we were praying. You see, when we stand as watchmen and gatekeepers in our territories, measures of rule and spheres of authority, the enemy can be hindered and prevented from establishing a foothold.

Greater Works than These

Now some of us might still feel skeptical about the authority given to us as sons and daughters of God. But the truth of the matter is, Jesus said we would do even greater works than He did! "I assure you, most solemnly I tell you, if anyone steadfastly believes in Me, he will himself be able to do the things that I do; and he will do even greater things than these, because I go to the Father" (John 14:12, AMP).

What an incredible promise from the Lord! As Jesus ascended to the throne room and the right hand of the Father, the Holy Spirit was sent to us. As believers we are empowered to do the work of the Kingdom of God. Upon receiving our orders from our King, we have the right and power of jurisdiction to execute them in our personal lives, in the lives of others, in our measure of rule, in creation and in the spiritual realm against the ranks of darkness.

I want to conclude this chapter with the powerful revelation Paul gives us concerning believers:

[For I always pray to] the God of our Lord Jesus Christ, the Father of glory, that He may grant you a spirit of wisdom and revelation [of insight into mysteries and secrets] in the [deep and intimate] knowledge of Him, by having the eyes of your heart flooded with light, so that you can know and understand the hope to which He has called you, and how rich is His glorious inheritance in the saints (His set-apart ones), and [so that you can know and understand] what is the immeasurable and unlimited and surpassing greatness of His power in and for us who believe, as demonstrated in the working of His mighty strength, which He exerted in Christ when He raised Him from the dead and seated Him at His [own] right hand in the heavenly [places], far above all rule and authority and power and dominion and every name that is named [above every title that can be conferred], not only in this age and in this world, but also in the age and the world which are to come. And He has put all things under His feet and has appointed Him the universal and supreme Head of the church [a headship exercised throughout the church],which is His body, the fullness of Him Who fills all in all [for in that body lives the full measure of Him Who makes everything complete, and Who fills everything every-where with Himself].

Ephesians 1:17–23, AMP

We are the Church, His Body, the fullness of Him who fills all in all. It is difficult to fathom the great and awesome inheritance made available to us. With Paul may we pray that the Lord give each of us a Spirit of wisdom and reve-lation and that the eyes of our hearts may be enlightened to the hope to which we have been called and the glorious inheritance with which we have been bestowed.

9

❀❀❀❀❀❀❀❀❀❀❀❀❀❀❀❀❀❀❀❀❀❀❀❀

WALKING IN PERMISSION

We see that, above all else, the keys to walking in effectiveness in our lives and spheres of influence are humility and
obedience to the Lord's plans. It is in hearing His voice
and direction that we are empowered to execute His purposes. Jesus showed us the way. In His ministry on earth, He
taught and performed what He saw the Father doing. He
told His disciples, "My Father is always at his work to this
very day, and I, too, am working. . . . I tell you the truth,
the Son can do nothing by himself; he can do only what
he sees his Father doing, because whatever the Father does
the Son also does" (John 5:17, 19). What is the work of

the Father that extends "to this very day"? The business of the Father is sustaining creation. Jesus kept Himself true to His Father's example.

It is necessary for us to grasp the idea that Jesus did not work independently of the Father. He understood that He could do nothing unless His Father was already doing it. We can compare this to human relationships: We have all seen sons who look like and act like their fathers. They model what has been modeled to them. Jesus, however, was relaying the idea that His relationship with His Father was on a higher level than that of a natural father/son relationship. While He was imitating His Father's actions, He was also working in agreement and perfect harmony with His Father.

Jesus knew the Father's fixed intent and purpose, completely and absolutely, because it was His intent and purpose as well. In this revelation Jesus pronounced a powerful message: He was stating that He has no differing, opposite or uncooperative plans, selfish ambitions or motives of His own. Nor does the Father have a will that is contrary to the Son's desires. They act in complete accord in their natures, plans, purposes and actions.

Jesus was fully God, but He was also fully man. In His human nature He had to learn to walk in the fullness of His purpose. In order to do so, He had to pull away from the crowds, pray, seek the Lord, hear His voice, advance in His calling in unity with the plans of His Father and overcome the schemes of the enemy unleashed against Him. Jesus and His Father worked together in restoring, reestablishing and extending the Kingdom of God in creation. Actually, what Jesus is explaining here is what we discussed in chapter 7: He did not "let go and let God," He "got in there with God."

How Does This Apply to Us?

This is the model for us as the ambassadors of the Kingdom of God. We, too, are to advance in permission, meaning we do what we see the Father doing. We, too, have to walk in accord with our Father through the guidance of the Holy Spirit. We, too, have to execute God's Kingdom plans and agendas in our lives, purpose and measure of rule. In other words, we listen for and obey the voice of our Father instead of presumptuously asking Him to bless our man-made ambitions.

As followers of Jesus we have many wonderful ideas, desires and visions that we feel certain will bless the Lord. But we have to consider: Have we prayed and sought the Lord concerning His pleasure in these plans, or have we jumped into action with our own programs and then asked God to bless them? You see, when we begin to think in terms of the Kingdom of God, we begin to see a bigger picture. Our focus becomes God's focus, and our plans, visions and dreams become His plans, visions and dreams. In this sense we partner together. Even in terms of spiritual authority, we will no longer be trapped in the practice of flexing our spiritual muscles expecting there to be a breakthrough. Just because we make a confession of dominion, this does not necessarily mean that authority and power have been released. When we line up with God and advance in His marching orders, we will walk in Kingdom authority and see breakthrough and transformation.

After my experience of first encountering the Holy Spirit, which I told you about in chapter 3, I began spending long hours in prayer and worship before the Lord. I had a hunger to know Him even more.

Greg and I were preparing to move to Houston. We arrived in town on a house-hunting trip and met up with Alice Smith, a close family friend and a highly successful real estate agent at the time. Alice told us that she had lined up for us to attend a large meeting that night in the Summit, a convention center that holds thousands of people. A world-renowned evangelist would be speaking. We were excited at this: The evangelist was the author of the book containing the prayer that had been the springboard for miraculously changing my life.

Alice knew that Greg and I had never attended a gathering like this. She spoke of how powerful the service the night before had been. She said it was time to lay down all skepticism and to trust God. By the time we arrived, we were both eager for the service to begin.

As the worship leader and choir led us in songs of adoration to the Lord, the presence that had become so sweet and real to me some twelve weeks before began to flood the convention center. It was a strong and precious presence. What an anointed time of exalting the Lord! The speaker gave a powerful message, and many people came forward for prayer and were healed.

As he was closing the service, this minister said that he felt the Lord leading him to pray an "impartation" to those who wanted more of God's presence. He gave this instruction: "Those of you who want this, put your hands up and get ready to receive." Without hesitation I threw my hands up to receive from the Lord. As soon as I did, I began to tremble at the touch of the Holy Spirit.

Alice noticed what was happening and quickly came to my side. "Becca," she asked, "do you need a healing?"

I said no.

"Well," she said, "this is obviously the Lord, so we are going to go with it." There were no arguments from me.

The minister extended his hands toward the audience to impart the anointing and exclaimed three times, "Take it, take it, take it!" Well, all I can say is, every time he spoke those words, it felt as if a bolt of lightning shot through my body. We were a great distance from the platform—up in the nosebleed section—but I might as well have been on the stage. By the third command, I fell backward onto the floor and was instantly swept away in the Spirit.

I no longer knew anything of my physical surroundings. I was clueless that I was on the floor, and if I had known I would not have cared. In the Spirit I had been taken to the throne room of God and was lying facedown at the feet of Jesus and our Father. The presence was glorious, awesome. I could see their feet, but their presence was so holy I stayed on my face and dared not move.

It is difficult to put into words what I felt. It was everything I could ever desire. I wept and sobbed as I lay at Jesus' feet and began to say, "Lord, this is all I have ever wanted in my life. You are awesome, powerful, wonderful and holy. Lord, please let me stay here with You. Don't send me back."

The Lord replied, *Becca, you must go back. You have a husband and daughter, and you will have more children. You have a call on your life that I have given you. I brought you here into My throne room to call you to Me and for you to understand the reality and revelation of who I am. I wanted you to experience the throne room of God. Now go fulfill your call.*

I wanted to stay, but the Lord had other plans that He revealed to me. I was not thinking that the Lord gave me that experience for a purpose until He told me the purpose. That experience was preparing me for my Kingdom role.

In this process of discovering and fulfilling our Kingdom roles, we must learn the difference between walking in the Spirit and walking in the soul. As we move in the Spirit, we operate in divinely authorized permission and will see fruit and a spiritual harvest. We will see Kingdom results.

A person who is submitted to the Spirit of the Lord will be characterized by obedience, humility, integrity, love for the Lord, love for one another and spiritual fruit.

When we function in the soul, however, we are depending on our own strength, and there is no life in our work. A person who is soul-led is focused on selfish desires, ambitions, traditions. That person is thinking on things of men and the world. Many times there will be control issues, and there is usually no lasting effect.

Now some of us are wondering this: *Will I get it right 100 percent of the time?* Probably not. The next question is: *Will God be upset if I miss it?* The answer to this question is also no. God looks at the motives of the heart. Our point here is that we all need to come to a place of understanding concerning our position with the Lord, the assignments and purposes He has given us and the divine destiny we have as Kingdom ambassadors in the earth. We all play a role in God's Kingdom plan in creation. It is time to get involved in walking out that plan—even if we have to begin with baby steps. We just start stewarding and managing God's Kingdom agendas. It is time to advance.

Peter and Kingdom Living

I enjoy reading about Peter in the gospels. He gives us so many examples of bringing the human nature in step with Jesus' purposes for creation. At times he spoke out of human reasoning and acted out of human emotion. He wept bitter tears of disgrace and grief, for instance, at having denied Jesus at our Lord's most difficult time in His ministry on earth. Yet at the same time, Peter was the one who revealed the true identity of Jesus. He understood who Jesus was. He walked on water and observed the Transfiguration. And we read in Acts 2 that after the Holy Spirit fell on the 120 in the Upper Room, Peter was the first to proclaim the Good News of Jesus Christ. By that one sermon three thousand people were saved! From that point he followed the Lord powerfully to the end of his life.

Response to the Transfiguration

Peter was driven, passionate and full of faith—and all too human. I think one of the reasons I enjoy studying his life is that he is easy to relate to. I usually find myself chuckling inside because I recognize that many times I react in the same headstrong and misguided manner. For the sake of our study concerning human desires, emotions and plans, let's investigate Peter's response to the Transfiguration. Keep in mind that this supernatural event occurred about a week after Peter's confession that Jesus was the Son of the living God. We will look comparatively in a moment at his quite different response to the Upper Room experience.

Now about eight days after these teachings, Jesus took with Him Peter and John and James and went up on the mountain to pray. And as He was praying, the appearance of His countenance became altered (different), and His raiment became dazzling white [flashing with the brilliance of lightning]. And behold, two men were conversing with Him—Moses and Elijah, who appeared in splendor and majesty and brightness and were speaking of His exit [from life], which He was about to bring to realization at Jerusalem. Now Peter and those with him were weighed down with sleep, but when they fully awoke, they saw His glory (splendor and majesty and brightness) and the two men who stood with Him. And it occurred as the men were parting from Him that Peter said to Jesus, Master, it is delightful and good that we are here; and let us construct three booths or huts—one for You and

157

one for Moses and one for Elijah! not noticing or knowing
what he was saying.

Luke 9:28–33, AMP

Now, the Transfiguration was a miraculous event, and there
are many powerful teachings we can glean from this occurrence. But our focus will be on Peter's reaction to it.

Jesus often sought times of seclusion. He would go to
the mountains for purposes of praying and spending time
with His Father. As the time drew near for the crisis in
Gethsemane and Calvary, He needed strength for His mission. Taking Peter, James and John with Him one day, He
climbed the mountain. While praying there, Jesus went
through a metamorphosis—we might think of a caterpil-
lar becoming a butterfly. His body was transformed into a
form of glory. Not only was Jesus transformed, but Moses
and Elijah appeared in glory and majesty and spoke with
Him about the approaching crucifixion and Jesus' exit
from this life. Moses, as we noted earlier, represented the
old covenant, and Elijah was the voice of the prophet
representing the new. Their presence testified that Jesus
was the true Messiah.

As Peter, James and John awoke from their sleep, they
witnessed the event. Why were they chosen to be with Jesus
at this moment? Maybe because they were more spiritually
advanced; maybe because they needed to learn spiritual lessons; maybe their faith needed to be strengthened for the
troubles they would face in the days ahead. One thing for
certain is the fact that they were average, uneducated men
who had the unprecedented privilege to follow Jesus and
witness firsthand His incredible teachings, miracles and love.
This experience would have served to confirm the truth of
Peter's confession that Jesus was the Christ.

Now I can imagine that these men were overwhelmed by what they saw. Even though Peter was not invited to be part of the conversation with the three figures before him, he jumped right in, making a suggestion to Jesus as Moses and Elijah were leaving. He wanted to delay their departure. Maybe he thought that this was the coming of the Messianic Age. Or maybe he thought he had "arrived" based on his earlier declaration that Jesus was the Son of the living God. Nevertheless, he blurted that it was good for him and the two other disciples to be there because they could build three huts, or tents, or dwellings. What Peter had in mind was a place where they could contain the holy atmosphere he felt on the Mount of Transfiguration.

As we read in verse 34, Peter did not know what he was saying. In other words, he was speaking foolishly out of his human emotions and desires. He was not operating in the Spirit but in his soul. Being so influenced by the awesome appearance of Moses and Elijah, he wanted them to stay so that he could continue to bask in this spiritual high.

You see, Peter had in mind the traditions of men. His reaction was to manufacture more of what man had always done. He was not thinking in terms of the Kingdom of God. Jesus was there to restore and bring the Kingdom to all mankind, but Peter wanted to stay on the mountaintop with Jesus and the prophets.

Isn't this similar to how we react when God moves supernaturally? We impulsively build our own plans and agendas around the event instead of asking the Lord for the purpose of the experience. But the Kingdom of God is not based on a place, building or dwelling—and particularly not one of man's own making. The Kingdom of God is everywhere and made known wherever we serve as Kingdom representatives.

This encounter that the disciples had with Jesus was preparing them for their Kingdom roles. I can relate to the tendency to react with human nature and desires because of my experience at the feet of Jesus. The desire for more of God is right and good. We should above all else seek His Kingdom and righteousness. We should always want more of Him and His supernatural realm. As we receive more of Him, however, our responses should build on God's blueprints and not our own. You see, like Peter I thought it was all about me; the truth of the matter is, it is all about God and His Kingdom.

Peter was learning, but he had not made the connection to Kingdom thinking. Not until the Upper Room experience when Jesus baptized His followers in the fire of the Holy Spirit.

In Comes the Holy Spirit

When we view the lives of the apostles before the Upper Room experience, we see them in a process of asking questions, discovering and learning. They were firsthand witnesses of Jesus—the form of man representing the fullness of the Kingdom of God. They observed and participated in many supernatural events, but they were not exhibiting Kingdom living. After the Holy Spirit came on them, these men and women were filled with holy boldness. Their understanding of the Kingdom of God changed, and they entered into their roles as Kingdom ambassadors. Peter—blunt, well-intentioned, all-too-human Peter—was no exception.

In truth, as we study Peter we discover that he was often the first of the disciples to stumble into this new kind of living, although he sometimes took two steps forward and one step back. He was the first to realize that Jesus was the Son of the living God; he was the first and only one to walk on water; he was the first to deny Jesus; he was the first disciple to the tomb after Mary brought the news that Jesus had risen from the dead; he was the first to preach the Gospel message; he was the first to preach to the Gentiles. Peter was on the forefront of all that was happening.

When the Holy Spirit came on the 120, they began to operate under His guidance and anointing. They now had the power of the Holy Spirit available in their lives. Their focus shifted from lack of understanding, blinding trust in tradition and selfish thinking to a Kingdom mindset of saving souls and influencing society. This time Peter never even considered the idea of stopping and building a dwelling to house the experience. Instead he began immediately to declare the Gospel.

We see his changed nature in the story told in Acts 10 and 11 of how God used Peter to bring salvation to the Gentiles. Cornelius was a centurion in the Italian regiment in the town of Caesarea. The Bible tells us that he was a God-fearing man who gave generously to those in need. One afternoon he had a vision.

> He distinctly saw an angel of God, who came to him and said, "Cornelius!" Cornelius stared at him in fear. "What is it, Lord?" he asked. The angel answered, "Your prayers and gifts to the poor have come up as a memorial offering before God. Now send men to Joppa to bring back a man named Simon who is called Peter. He is staying with Simon the tanner, whose house is by the sea."
>
> Acts 10:3–6

Needless to say Cornelius dispatched two of his servants and a devout soldier who was one of his attendants to find this man Simon.

As they were on their journey and nearing the city, Peter went up on the roof to pray. The Spirit caused him to fall into a trance and he, too, had a vision. "He saw heaven opened and something like a large sheet being let down to earth by its four corners. It contained all kinds of four-footed animals, as well as reptiles of the earth and birds of the air. Then a voice told him, 'Get up, Peter. Kill and eat'" (verses 11–13).

Peter was aghast at that suggestion: "Surely not, Lord! . . . I have never eaten anything impure or unclean" (verse 14).

Peter was sensitive to the Spirit and the voice of the Lord, but his lifestyle of obedience to the Law was still in force, and it was overriding his desire to obey. In his human thinking, it was difficult for him to believe the Lord would say this to him. "The voice spoke to him a second time, 'Do not call anything impure that God has made clean.' This happened three times, and immediately the sheet was taken back to heaven" (verses 15–16).

The Lord was using this vivid picture to prepare Peter for his Kingdom role of bringing salvation to the Gentiles. Peter had enough discernment to understand that the vision was symbolic and began pondering the interpretation. About that time the three men sent by Cornelius stopped at the gate of his house asking for him. The Spirit then spoke to Peter: "Simon, three men are looking for you. So get up and go downstairs. Do not hesitate to go with them, for I have sent them" (verses 19–20). The vision required an act of obedience by Peter, and the Spirit led him step-by-step.

The visitors were welcomed into the home, whereupon they stated their business. The next day they all set out for Caesarea along with a group of men from Joppa. Peter knew he would be called into question for going to a Gentile home and so took witnesses he could depend on.

Now Cornelius was expecting them, even though he knew it was against Jewish law for a Jewish person to associate with a Gentile. Not only was it illegal, it was also an offensive and detestable notion to the Jews. But Cornelius sent for his relatives and close friends to be part of the amazing thing that God was doing. As Peter entered the home and saw the crowd, he explained that God had told him to come, for he must no longer call any man impure. He then asked why he had been summoned.

Cornelius described the encounter he had had with the angel of God and explained that he, his family and friends were eager to hear everything the Lord had commanded Peter to tell them. Peter then shared a landmark message in the history of the Early Church. This sermon is important because in it Peter revealed that he now fully understood the meaning of the rooftop vision: God is no respecter of persons; He does not show favoritism or partiality.

When Peter recognized that God sent him to share the truth of Jesus Christ, he realized that his purpose and measure of rule was to break cultural beliefs, traditions and prejudices between Jew and Gentile and open the door for all mankind to hear the truth of the Gospel.

Peter was operating under the mandate of the Lord, and because of his obedience there were powerful results. As he preached, the Holy Spirit came on all who heard the message. The Jewish believers who came with Peter were astonished that the gift of the Holy Spirit had been poured out on the Gentiles! Could this really be in God's plan? Then Peter confounded their thinking further: "Can anyone keep these people from being baptized with water? They have received the Holy Spirit just as we have" (verse 47). He ordered that they be baptized in the name of Jesus Christ.

It did not take long for the news to spread throughout Judea. When Peter left there and traveled to Jerusalem, the Jewish believers began immediately to criticize him. Peter explained everything that had happened and concluded with

163

these words: "If God gave them the same gift as he gave us, who believed in the Lord Jesus Christ, who was I to think that I could oppose God?" (Acts 11:17).

No one could doubt that God had been at work. When the Jewish believers heard the truth, they had no further objections and began to praise God that even the Gentiles could receive repentance unto life.

What a tremendous encounter! This incident changed the face of Christianity in the Early Church and, through those believers, throughout the world today. When we operate under the direction of our own understanding, traditions and human desires, we can miss the big picture and God's designed plan. However, when we walk in step with our Savior, operate under the anointing of the Holy Spirit and embrace His direction, we will see and respond to the Kingdom plan of God and transformation will take place.

Making an Impact

It is amazing to think that our Father is always focused on His work of redeeming creation. This is the message for us as the ambassadors of the Kingdom of God. We, too, must walk in permission and do what we see the Father doing. Let me repeat: We all have the same Holy Spirit operating through us that Peter did. Now, I know we all might not be called to be a Peter. Even so, we can have an impact where God has placed us now and everywhere we go. We are called to have dominion!

10

REIGNING IN LIFE

Our God is an awesome, powerful, faithful God who created each of us to walk in dominion and shine as Kingdom ambassadors. Paul gives us an incredible positional truth in Romans 5:17: "For if, by the trespass of the one man, death reigned through that one man, how much more will those who receive God's abundant provision of grace and of the gift of righteousness reign in life through the one man, Jesus Christ."

Paul does not say that life reigns over us. Nor does he say that life reigns in us. He does say that we shall reign in life! Here are definitions for *basileuo*, the Greek word for *reign*: "to be king, to exercise kingly power, to govern a province, to exercise the highest influence, to control." As I studied this verse, I discovered that this great promise of Romans 5:17 can be translated word by word into the following expounded interpretation:

> If one man's one offense let loose against us the tyrant power of Death, to hold us as its victims in helpless bondage, much more, when we stand forth enriched with God's abounding grace and in the beauty of complete absolution (forgiveness, pardon, release, freedom, liberty) from countless offenses, shall we increase in a life divinely owned and legally secured, reigning (exercising the highest influence and kingly power, governing a province) in exultant freedom and unchallenged might, through that other matchless One, Jesus Christ!

> Robert Jamieson, A. R. Fausset, and David Brown,
> *A Commentary, Critical and Explanatory, on the
> Old and New Testaments* (Oak Harbor, Wash.:
> Logos Research Systems, Inc., 1997), 2.

Wow! What a powerful promise from the Word of God! I want us to examine one final example from the life of Paul that we can apply to our lives. It is located in Ephesians 6:19–20: "Pray also for me, that whenever I open my mouth, words may be given me so that I will fearlessly make known the mystery of the gospel, for which I am an ambassador in chains. Pray that I may declare it fearlessly, as I should."

During the writing of the book of Ephesians, Paul was imprisoned in Rome for proclaiming the Gospel message. Even while being held prisoner, Paul continued to make known and decree his faith in Jesus through his writings to the Church. I have been to Rome and have stood and prayed in the underground prison cell where Paul was kept before his death. It was a small, wet, cold, dark, cavelike cell with floors and walls of stone. It would have been a distressing place to stay for any length of time. Yet from this place, Paul wrote this book and other books of the Bible from an overflow of his prayer life.

I find it inspiring that as he closed the letter to the church of Ephesus, Paul did not ask for them to pray for his release or his personal needs. While I am sure there were times that Paul did pray for his own needs, he was more focused on prayers for boldness. He needed the enablement and strength of the Holy Spirit that he might continue to proclaim the truth of the Gospel fearlessly, boldly and frankly. Here is a thought: Maybe we believers would receive more answers to prayer if we followed Paul's example of not focusing on self, negative circumstances, hindrances and weaknesses, but, instead, prayed more for the enablement of the Lord in our lives to proclaim the Gospel and to influence the territories to which we are assigned.

Paul had every right to be afraid in his circumstances, and I am sure there were times he was overwhelmed. Every time he declared the Good News of the redemption from sins, he was increasing the chance of punishment by death. It is hard even to imagine. Even so, Paul knew his position as a Kingdom ambassador for which he was held a prisoner in chains. He understood he was a special appointee of Jesus Christ Himself. He was speaking for the Lord as His representative. He was determined, therefore, to speak out with boldness no matter the cost.

As disciples of Jesus we need to learn from Paul's example. We cannot allow our fears to hold us back. Brothers and sisters, we must advance the Kingdom of God. As the Body of Christ we have to move out of a condition of fear and into our rightful position of boldness and authority. This is not a time to shrink back, but to move forward. Fear has to go!

We have been too long on the defense instead of the offense. As I was praying the other day, the Lord showed me a picture of what we have been studying in this book. Now this is a simple analogy, but I want to share it as it will give us encouragement and understanding.

I saw a football game. The two teams were lined up at the line of scrimmage preparing for the ball to be snapped. One team wore black uniforms and the other white. The team with white uniforms was the Lord's team, and the team with black uniforms was Satan's. At the beginning of the game the white-uniform team had possession of the ball, but fumbled. The black-uniform team recovered the ball and began to run plays that were winning the game.

At one point the ball was intercepted by one member of the white-uniform team, but it was as if his team members did not know it had changed hands. So even though the ball was rightfully theirs, they continued to allow the black-uniform team to run offense. The white-uniform team focused only on defending its territory, as though expecting to be on the defense.

But all of a sudden the white-uniform team seemed to realize that the ball had been theirs and that the other team had possession only because they had handed it over voluntarily. They decided that enough was enough. On the next play they intercepted the ball confidently! Not only that, the player with the ball ran so quickly to the end zone that the other team could not catch him. The white-uniform team left the black-uniform team in the dust to win the game.

Friends, we are the white team. Yes, the ball was forfeited by Adam and Eve, but Jesus intercepted it. The enemy continues to have illegal possession of the ball because we allow him to. The truth is, we are so busy in the defensive mode that we do not realize we have the right to grab that ball and run the offense. Not only are we to call the plays, but we are to run with confidence, assurance, faith and authority.

As we said earlier, when we rise out of bed in the morning, darkness should come to attention. We are the ones who should call the offensive play of the day that will end with a victory in the end zone. We have to shift our thinking from *What do we have to defend ourselves from today?* to living each day focused on God, His plans and His agendas. We praise Him for His goodness. We expect to see individuals, families, workplaces, cities and nations transformed for the glory of God.

> Therefore then, since we are surrounded by so great a cloud of witnesses [who have borne testimony to the Truth], let us strip off and throw aside every encumbrance (unnecessary weight) and that sin which so readily (deftly and cleverly) clings to and entangles us, and let us run with patient endurance and steady and active persistence the appointed course of the race that is set before us, looking away [from all that will distract] to Jesus, Who is the Leader and the Source of our faith [giving the first incentive for our belief] and is also its Finisher [bringing it to maturity and perfection]. He, for the joy [of obtaining the prize] that was set before Him, endured the cross, despising and ignoring the shame, and is now seated at the right hand of the throne of God.
>
> Hebrews 12:1–2, AMP

Friends, we were created for dominion. We are Kingdom ambassadors. Everywhere we are, the Kingdom of God is also there. Creation is waiting with eager expectation. Souls are awaiting salvation. God has given each of us a responsibility, a purpose, a measure of rule. This is the season and this is the time to determine to run the race set before us and take our rightful places. We are destined to rule in life with the King of kings and the Lord of lords.

Let's move into our rightful position as righteous sons and daughters establishing the dominion standard for which we were made. "Then the righteous will shine like the sun in the kingdom of their Father" (Matthew 13:43). And all creation will see.

INDEX

Rebecca Greenwood, cofounder and president of Christian Harvest International, serves as an ordained minister to the Body of Christ. An internationally known speaker, she conducts seminars and conferences on numerous topics including prayer, intercession, spiritual warfare, spiritual mapping, deliverance and prophecy. She also equips believers with scriptural truths on living lives of purpose, fulfillment and destiny.

Over the past fifteen years, she has led and participated in spiritual warfare prayer journeys to seventeen countries and to many cities throughout the United States. She has seen thousands of individuals saved, set free and healed.

She and her husband, Greg, served for six years with Eddie and Alice Smith at the U.S. Prayer Center. During this time, she served as prayer coordinator of Houston House of Prayer and the U.S. Prayer Center, where she led prayer meetings and initiatives, the deliverance ministry and ministry teams.

Rebecca served with Peter and Doris Wagner of Global Harvest Ministries for four years. She functioned as manager of the Arsenal Bookstore, located in the World Prayer Center, and as executive assistant to Peter and Doris. During this time she received a Bachelor's of Practical Ministry diploma from Wagner Leadership Institute.

She is a member of the International Society of Deliverance Ministers Founders Circle under the direction of Peter and Doris Wagner, and the Women in Strategic Leadership Roundtable and Global Leadership Network led by Naomi Dowdy. She serves on the Change the World School of Prayer teaching faculty in conjunction with Dick Eastman of Every Home for Christ. Rebecca also teaches for Wagner Leadership Institute in Colorado Springs, Colorado, and abroad.

Published works include *Authority to Tread: An Intercessor's Guide to Strategic-Level Spiritual Warfare* and *Breaking the Bonds of Evil: How to Set People Free from Demonic Oppression*, as well as an e-book, *The Power of a Godly Mother*. She has also written articles regarding prayer for *SpiritLed Woman* and has contributed to articles in *Charisma* and *Pray!* magazines.

Rebecca and Greg, who serves as director of church partnerships for Every Home for Christ, reside in Colorado Springs, Colorado. They have three beautiful daughters, Kendall, Rebecca and Katie.

To contact Rebecca Greenwood to speak or minister at your event, or for more information about Christian Harvest International, please contact:

Christian Harvest International
P.O. Box 63628
Colorado Springs, CO 80962
(719) 243-3302
info@christianharvestintl.org
www.christianharvestintl.org